So Simple

upholstery

CRE▲TIVE
HOMEOWNER®

So Simple
upholstery

CRE🏠TIVE
HOMEOWNER®

First Published in North America in 2005 by

CRE▲TIVE
HOMEOWNER®

Creative Homeowner® is a registered trademark of
Federal Marketing Corporation

Copyright © 2005 PRC Publishing

International Standard Book Number : 1-58011-238-2
Library of Congress Catalog Card Number: 2004114554

Current printing (last digit)
10 9 8 7 6 5 4 3 2 1

Produced by PRC Publishing
The Chrysalis Building
Bramley Road, London W10 6SP,
United Kingdom

An imprint of **Chrysalis** Books Group plc

Printed and bound in China

CREATIVE HOMEOWNER
A Division of Federal Marketing Corp.
24 Park Way
Upper Saddle River, NJ 07458

www.creativehomeowner.com

Picture Acknowledgments
All images © Chrysalis Image Library apart from the
following:
T=Top B= Bottom C= Center R = Right L=Left.

© Chrysalis Image Library / Simon Clay: 3, 6, 7, 22C, 60B,
65, 66B, 73, 84B, 93, 94B, 107, 108B, 123, 124B, 133.
© Chrysalis Image Library / Mark Franklin: 24R, 42.
© Crowson, www.crowsonfabrics.com (UK)(01825 761055)
/ Monkwell, www.monkwell.com (UK)(01825 747901): 2,
5, 8, 9, 10, 11, 13, 14, 17, 18, 20, 20 (inset), 21T, 22T.
© www.leatherstudio.co.uk 19B, 22B.

CONTENTS

INTRODUCTION

SKILLS, SPACE, AND TIME

We've all got a set of dining chairs that could do with some attention or a sofa that would look so much better covered in a fabric more in keeping with the new drapes. If you can find an upholsterer in your area, chances are he is busy for the next six months and deep down you'll feel that you're paying good money to have something done that you could probably do yourself.

A wing chair and matching footstool complement the curtains and decoration of this living room.

GETTING STARTED

Given the right tools and a little space you can save a lot of time, a lot of money, and learn a new skill by doing all but the most complicated household upholstery jobs yourself. It may take a little practice and a bit of courage and perseverance, but if you've got a sewing machine that you get out from time to time to raise the hem on a pair of trousers or run up some new drapes, and you pride yourself on your gift wrapping skills come Thanksgiving, you've almost certainly got all the natural skills you need to make a fine upholsterer.

If you've got those skills, this book will show you how to apply them to various different household upholstery projects. Chapter 2 gives a brief lesson on the various elements that go into upholstered furniture and cushions. Chapter 3 goes into some detail on the innumerable fabric choices that preoccupy every house proud upholsterer. Chapter 4

Sumptuous upholstery will lend any room a touch of elegance.

has an in depth look through the tools and techniques you will have to be familiar with, and then finally Chapter 5 shows step by step how to upholster eight different projects.

The projects start with a simple introduction to re-covering a straightforward style of chair. If you've got a set of dining chairs that you bought a few years back, chances are they could do with a change of fabric, either because the old covering is worn out or it just simply doesn't match up to your current tastes. Get yourself a good pair of scissors, a staple gun, and some new fabric and you're half way to a new looking set of chairs.

The drop in seat is a popular design of dining chair that has been around for more than 150 years. Upholstering a drop in seat chair is a good first introduction to the more skilled elements of traditional upholstery. It's a straightforward project that requires very little space as the seat pad is removed from the chair frame, but it will certainly test whether you've got the skills to take on more complicated projects.

The projects step up a gear with the T-cushion club chair. It's a classic design that fits well in the most

Upholstery gives you an opportunity to express different aspects of your personality and mood: whether it be elegantly restrained (left), or flamboyant, even passionate (above).

modern of settings. So if you've got an old chair like this it might just need a more modern fabric to give it a new lease on life. With any fully upholstered piece of furniture, you'll need to set aside some space and take your time, but the finished article will more than repay your investment.

The wing chair is a universally recognized design and a much sought after piece of furniture. This project is very similar to the club chair, but the addition of wings above the arms brings a little more complexity that requires a slightly different approach. The barrel or tub chair will challenge the hobbyist upholsterer with its inner curved face. The trick with this style of chair is to cover the inside arms and back with three pieces of fabric jointed in two places. This project will take you step by step through the process, so that you can apply the technique to other pieces with what can appear to be troublesome curves.

The nursing chair was chosen because it takes the concept of dealing with an inner curved face like the barrel chair and takes it one step further by deep buttoning it. The inner surface is still upholstered using three pieces of fabric, but this time the three pieces are invisibly joined using the technique of deep buttoning. Buttoning is a skill that draws admiration from all would-be upholsterers, but follow this project and you'll soon be reaching for the double ended needle and buttoning twine with confidence.

Obviously if you're going to tackle something as big as a sofa then you'll need a great deal more space than for a chair, but if you have the space then you'll find that a sofa is just a big chair. The upholstered settle sofa shows you how to re-upholster the type of couch that comes apart, and the loose cushion sofa shows you how to breathe new life into that comfy old couch you just cannot bear to throw away.

Upholstery isn't difficult, but you still need to start off with a fairly simple project just to find your feet. The first two projects in Chapter 5 are ideal chairs for any novice to start with; both are physically small so they won't take you too long to complete, won't cost too much for materials, and require little in the way of work space. If you don't have a simple dining chair, then you will probably know someone who has and who will be more than happy to give it to you. If not then second hand, antique, and junk

Raid junk stores for cheap bargains to transform (left). Imaginative use of textures can breathe new life into humble cushions (above).

stores are full of drop-in seat chairs that cost very little money.

Once you've got your chair, you'll need to set some space aside to work in and track down a few of the upholstery tools and materials listed in Chapter 4. Upholstery tool suppliers aren't that common, but the Internet is an excellent resource for tools and materials these days, especially for specialist items such as webbing stretchers and tack lifters. It's difficult when you first embark on a new hobby, because you have to spend money to acquire the tools you need to get started but you don't know whether you're going to enjoy the hobby or not. Fortunately, less than $100 will get you a basic tool kit. Once you make more of a commitment to upholstery, then you may want to invest in more expensive tools. But to start, inexpensive tools are perfectly adequate.

SAFETY

The first upholstery task you're likely to do is ripping off the old upholstery. You must be aware that old furniture accumulates a lot of dust and dirt. If you're working at home, lay a sheet down to protect the floor and wear a dust mask to protect your nose and lungs. Old tacks, and particularly staples, are very sharp so be very careful not to kneel on them when stripping furniture. Watch out when handling the furniture you're stripping as there are always going to be broken off staples ready to draw blood.

Goose neck webbing stretchers are particularly vicious tools as they have a row of sharp spikes used to grip the jute webbing with; hammers and mallets are always ready to bruise a clumsy hand or thumb. When using a tack lifter always force it away from your body and never have a hand in front of it supporting the furniture. The lifter will slip and end up in your hand, maybe not the first time you do it, but eventually and when you least expect it.

Other potential hazards you will come across are long sharp needles, sewing machines, and, if you're taking chairs that have been stored in a garage for a while, spiders and other critters. With upholstery, the pricked finger is inevitable, but serious injury isn't as long as you're careful, you take what you're doing seriously, and you maintain a safe work environment.

CHAPTER I

BASIC STYLES

VARIATIONS IN FURNITURE CONSTRUCTION

TIGHT BACK AND SEAT

Tight back and seat describes a style of chair or sofa that has neither seat nor back cushions. This form of construction provides a firm and supportive upholstery that was popular in the late 19th and early 20th centuries when chairs were used for activities such as reading, embroidery, and engaging in conversation. Tight back and seat furniture is firm but generally well padded, so that it is supportive without being too hard.

LOOSE AND ATTACHED CUSHIONS

The addition of seat and back cushions was a development from the tight back and seat style. Furniture with loose seat and back cushions has been around since the mid 19th century, but the invention of the radio followed by television in the 20th century heralded a change in people's attitude toward their seating arrangements. There was a move away from formal, firm seating and toward softer and more relaxing sofas and chairs. Furniture makers sprung seats and backs with shorter springs and used less padding to accommodate deep box cushions so that the sitter could sink into furniture, rather than sit upright on it. Loose cushion furniture remains the prevailing style of most modern furniture.

Above: A classic sofa from the 1930s is upholstered in cut velvet and shows the decorative wood detail and split back design typical of the art deco period.

Left: Split back syles, though first seen a hundred or more years ago, are still popular today.

SPLIT BACK STYLE

During the Art Deco period, the fashion was for sofas with backs that looked as if they had loose cushions but were incorporated into the upholstery. This style, known as split back, was again popular in the 1970s and still remains a common shape. Split back sofas combine the best elements of the tight back and box cushion seat style, so that the seats are soft and comfortable, and the backs provide more stable support.

Dark wood (left) and light wood (right) for furniture frames have taken turns to be in and out of favor for a century or more. Furniture designers have always been both followers of, and also creators of, prevailing fashions and styles. Whatever the style however, one of the constant joys for the upholsterer is the contrast and interplay between the hard frame and the soft material.

EXPOSED FRAME

From ornate, colonial bergere furniture with its woven cane infilling, to the common dining chair with a drop-in seat, many styles of sofas and chairs have elements of an exposed frame. You can tell what color and type of wood is in fashion at any given point in time by looking at the exposed frame furniture being produced. For example, dark, carved woods were popular in the late 19th century and plain, pale, bleached woods are often seen in modern Scandanavian styles.

Leather (below) makes its own particular demands on the upholsterer; but in some ways it makes life easier, in that the choice of pattern and texture are of course much more limited than they are for cloth (far left).

TUFTED

Tufting, also known as buttoning, is a traditional style of upholstery that gained popularity in the mid 19th century when leather hide became a popular furniture covering. The irregular shape and size of hide, and the fact that it is difficult to stitch together, necessitated the development of an upholstery style that incorporated hidden joins. The solution was the "Chesterfield" style of sofa with its low back, distinctive deep buttons, and diamond pattern folds. Tufting remains an essential technique for large areas of leather upholstery. Using either a shallow or deep tufting pattern, furniture makers incorporate its decorative effect in many different styles.

MODULAR OR SECTIONAL FURNITURE

Modular or sectional furniture comprises separate units, usually including a corner unit, which can be combined according to individual requirements. It ends with one arm and also includes a table or tables. This design only became possible with the advent of modern upholstery construction methods. It became very popular in the minimalist era of the 1970s, and is still popular today as a practical

solution to long seating areas in waiting rooms and offices.

CUSHION SHAPES

T-CUSHIONS

These seat or back cushions are shaped to fit around the front or over the tops of arms. "T" describes the shape of a seat cushion on a chair that fills the area of the seat, and the recesses in front of the arms. On a sofa with recessed arms and three seat cushions, the central cushion will be square and the two outer cushions will be "L" shaped. T-cushions come in two types: square ended and round shouldered.

Far left: Examples of square-ended T- cushions, the reason for the name is clearer on the armchair than on the sofa.

Left and below: Bolster cushions have a distinct period feel and come as something of a surprise with any piece of furniture that uses more modern patterns or colors.

TURKISH CUSHIONS

Turkish cushions are large floor cushions that traditionally have one or both sides covered in carpet.

BOLSTER CUSHIONS

Long, with flat ends and a round profile, bolster cushions are used predominantly as decoration on sofas and chaises with recessed or ornately shaped inner arms. They were very popular with furniture makers of the 19th century, but are not so common in modern times.

ARM SHAPES

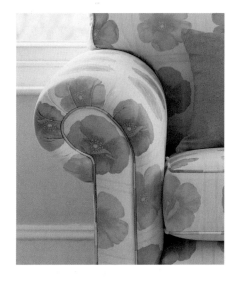

ROLLED ARM

The rolled arm is the most common and enduring shape for upholstered arms. Describing an arm with a rounded top, the term is used for both plain or elegant styles, with either flat or recessed fronts. The distinguishing feature of the rolled arm is that the front of the arm forms the shape of a scroll. A variation on the rolled arm is the inset panel, which was developed in line with modern upholstery methods to do away with the need to hand-stitch scrolls. It comprises a separate upholstered panel, which is applied to the front of the arm to neatly finish and cover the fabric ends.

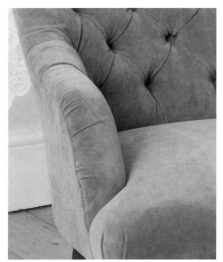

BRIDGEWATER ARM

With a padded inside face and flat outside, the Bridgewater is a simpler style of arm.

TUXEDO ARM

With its thin, squared-off style, the Tuxedo arm is found predominantly on modern styles of furniture including modular furniture from the 1970s onward. A Tuxedo arm is the same height as the back of the piece of furniture.

LEGS, FEET, AND SKIRTS

Legs are often the only wood exposed, and you can tell a lot from them about quality. This is particularly true of older furniture, indicating that a piece is an original or a reproduction. The twist turned legs and stretcher (left) were popular in the early 19th century.

TURNED LEGS

Popular from the earliest times, turned legs get their name and distinctive shape from being turned on a lathe. Traditionally terminating with a brass castor, they can be long and elegant or short and stocky, and can be found on all styles of furniture to the modern day. Good quality turned legs are a sign of a well-made, expensive piece of furniture.

PYRAMID LEGS

Pyramid-style legs became popular as an alternative to turned legs when fashion began to favor geometric designs during the Art Deco period of the early 20th century. Shaped like inverted pyramids, their popularity did not endure for long, though modern examples can still occasionally be seen.

CABRIOLE LEGS

A distinctive style of leg popular for many centuries, cabriole legs are also known as Queen Anne and can be plain or ornately carved. Cabriole legs from the Gothic Revival period were commonly carved with the foot in the shape of a claw holding a ball.

BUN FEET

This type of leg is also turned, but is distinctively short and plain, like a squashed ball. Bun feet can be flat bottomed or sometimes recessed so as to partly conceal a castor. This is another popular and enduring style that was prominent in the late 19th and early part of the 20th century and is still used today.

SKIRTS

Skirts are a way of extending the fabric of a chair or sofa down to the ground so that all legs and castors are covered. Good quality legs and castors are expensive and poor quality ones are better not seen, so modern styles have tended to incorporate skirts.

CHAPTER II

BASIC ANATOMY

The elements of a well-constructed piece of furniture include: the frame, deck construction (including coil springs and webbing), and the cushion content. This section shows how a piece of furniture is basically constructed.

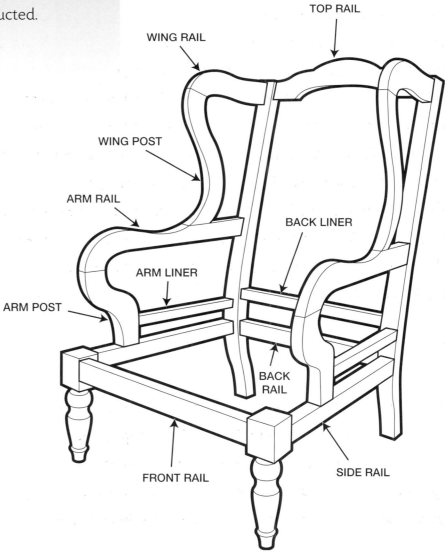

TOP RAIL

WING RAIL

WING POST

ARM RAIL

BACK LINER

ARM LINER

ARM POST

BACK RAIL

FRONT RAIL

SIDE RAIL

Standard upholstery materials include webbing, springs, Dacron, and muslin.

THE FRAME

The diagram (left) and photo (right) show the frame of a Victorian wing chair with Bridgewater arms. At the time when it was made, prior to mass production methods common from the 1930s onward, all furniture frames were constructed in the same manner. Strip any traditionally upholstered chair or sofa back to its hardwood frame and you will find variations in shape and style, but not in the basic construction principles. The foundation of all traditional upholstery is the seat frame, which is made of thicker rails than the rest of the construction, as is illustrated in the wing chair. It is on this base that the chair frame is added. Although

A Victorian wing chair frame with Bridgewater arms.

well made and sturdy, the main function of the frame is to form the shape of the finished chair. Even in its frame form, it is not difficult to imagine what the wing chair will look like once upholstered.

The upholsterer has a certain amount of licence with a frame, for example choosing whether to incorporate a box cushion in the seat or upholster it tight. The thickness of arms and the depth of the back can also be tailored to suit the customer. However, the basic shape of the finished chair is dictated by the frame. Some chairs—tub chairs in particular—of the same period had a frame made of iron, hence the name "iron back," but they too were attached to a sturdy hardwood seat base.

THE DECK

The picture shows the upturned wing chair frame with the jute webbing stretched tightly from side to side and top to bottom on its base. The jute is stretched with the use of a webbing stretcher. If you were to strike this webbing with the back of your hand, it would ring like a drum. It is this tension that pulls all

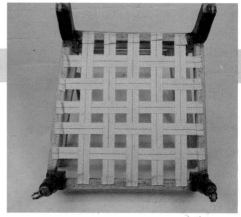

The deck distributes the sitter's weight.

the chair's joints together and provides its strength. A chair frame is only made strong and stable once the base is covered in webbing.

The next element in seat construction is the coil spring. A chair such as the wing chair would have at least nine seat springs stitched onto the webbed base, and these perform the main load bearing task. The coil springs are tied together so that their movement is coordinated and restricted to up and down. The springs act in unison to evenly distribute and disperse the weight of a seated person into the webbed base and out into the chair's frame and legs. Just like a well engineered bridge, weight and forces are distributed over a wide area so that no one piece of the chair's complex construction takes more weight than it can easily bear. This is, of course, only true while the chair's upholstery, and particularly the seat webbing, is in good condition; once the upholstery starts to degrade so does the chair's load bearing abilities.

A layer of burlap is stitched over the coil springs and secured to the top of the seat rails. It is over this

Coil springs can only do their job if stitched upright into the deck.

No springs, as on this settle frame, means much thicker rails.

that padding is added to make the desired shape and height of the deck. On a traditional chair, the stuffing would be of fiber or animal hair, and on a reproduction piece it would be modern foam. If a box cushion was to be incorporated in the seat, then the deck would be upholstered thinly to allow room, otherwise the deck would be upholstered to the required seat height.

The picture (above right) shows the seat frame of the upholstered bench, one of the projects in Chapter 5. The frame has been constructed to make it as strong as possible, but in order to achieve this, comfort has to be sacrificed: the wooden cross members that fill the seat rails make for a stronger base than webbing and springs, but also a much less forgiving one. The construction of all seating furniture is always a compromise between strength and comfort.

CUSHION FILLINGS

Cushions can be filled with a wide variety of materials (some old cushions even incorporate springs), but the three main types of filling that the upholsterer will come across are down, foam, and synthetic fiber.

DOWN

Down is a high quality feather taken from the chests of water birds such as goose, duck, and eider, and as such has the very good insulating and air trapping qualities that make it ideal for cushions. Down is expensive and is invariably mixed with inferior quality feathers to bulk it out. Unfortunately, poor quality feathers do not possess the same qualities as down. Cheap feather cushions quickly go flat and cannot be plumped up. The down in cushions needs to be contained in a feather-proof inner casing made of glazed closely woven material such as cambric or ticking.

From the bottom up: foam wrapped in Dacron, synthetic fiber, down, and shaped high density foam.

FOAM

Manmade synthetic foam cushion fillings are the most common these days. High density foam is often preformed into exactly the required shape for the cushion and has excellent wear qualities, which means it can be inserted into a cushion cover directly without the need for any wrapping or lining. Lower density and older foam cushion inners are less hard-wearing and will often be wrapped in a protective Dacron wrapping to prevent the outside from crumbling and being worn away by the abrasive underside of the cushion cover.

SYNTHETIC FIBER

Not as dense and shaped as foam, but of a more reliable quality, durability, and affordability than down, synthetic fiber is an excellent compromise filling for cushions. Often, a loose cushion sofa will incorporate the density and durability of foam cushions on the seat, and soft synthetic fiber cushions on the back. Synthetic fiber must be contained within an inner cover, though it doesn't need to be made of anything special. Synthetic fiber inners can be bought ready made to fit most sizes of cushion cover.

CHAPTER III

FABRICS AND TRIMMINGS

FABRICS

Walk into any soft furnishing or fabric shop and you'll be overwhelmed with choice. However, before you get carried away, remember that the primary consideration in choosing a fabric for a furniture project is that it is suitable for upholstery as opposed to, say, drapes or dressmaking: after all it will be sat on every day for a number of years. Each of the fabrics on show should have a label to indicate its suitability for a particular purpose. This may be written either in words or symbols. The symbol to look out for is a basic line drawing of a sofa or chair. This section is a guide to some common upholstery fabric types.

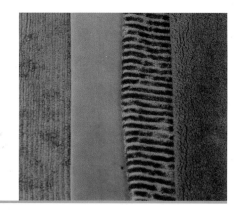

Velvet (above and above right) can be made of various materials— silk, cotton, linen, polyester—but its main distinguishing feature is its distinctive short dense pile. Depending on what it is made from, velvet ranges from delicate to extremely hard wearing, so not all are suitable for upholstery. Check the label!

Velvet is extremely versatile and always an excellent choice for upholstery. It is used in all styles and is available in many variations, including with shapes and patterns cut into the pile (known as cut velvet) and printed fake animal skins, which are sometimes used to cover up staple and tack heads at the bottom of furniture.

Aside from cuts and prints, corded and crushed velvets (above) ensure that there is a velvet suitable for just about any upholstery project.

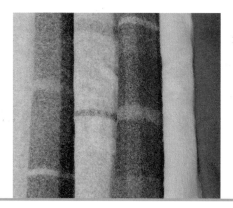

Chenile (above) is another fabric with a distinctive pile. This fabric is an excellent choice for the upholsterer wanting to cover a large piece of furniture, as it is cheaper to produce than most quality velvets, comes in a huge range of styles and textures, and is generally thick and hard wearing.

Wool (above) is a fabric familiar to all. There are some beautiful wool upholstery fabrics available, but these tend to be more expensive than other materials. And with few designs other than plain colors and tartan to choose from, it provides a limited palette for the upholsterer.

Moquette (above) was used extensively in upholstery and in train and coach seats from the 1930s until the late 1960s, when it fell out of fashion. It has a carpet-like roughness that makes it extremely hard wearing. A recent revival in retro styles has seen it return to many fabric shops.

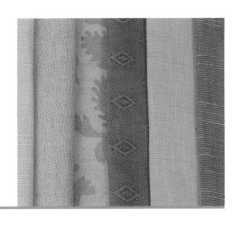

Damask (above) can be made from a number of natural and synthetic materials. Its distinguishing feature is that the pattern is woven into the fabric rather than being printed on. Damasks are found in the whole price range of upholstery fabrics, with cost depending on what the fabric is made from.

Silk (above) is often, and rightly, regarded as an expensive and decadent choice of upholstery fabric. However, silk and synthetic mixes give the same look and texture at a reasonable price. With its distinctive sheen, silk is a thin fabric and should be used for showpiece furniture rather than heavily used pieces.

Linen (above) is a hard-wearing natural fiber with a slightly rough texture. Suitable for all types of upholstery, linen often has printed designs and is also available with a glazed finish.

Prints (above) can be applied to any fabric and cotton prints are among the cheapest upholstery materials available. Make sure that what you are buying is suitable to the furniture and that the design is one that will complement the room. Also think carefully about whether the design is one you can live with for a long time.

Stripes (above) are not suitable for all shapes and designs of furniture. Before you buy a striped fabric for a piece of furniture think about whether you intend to button it, or whether it has flamboyant curves or other unusual features. Striped fabric may look ideal on the roll, but any inaccuracy in applying it will be amplified.

TRIMMINGS

Trimmings are generally used to finish off fabric edges; hide tacks, staples, and seams; and give a professional appearance. You can easily buy ready-made trimmings such as braid, gimp, and decorative cord colored to complement your fabric, or if you prefer to create something that will match perfectly, piping can be made from the same fabric that you are using to cover the piece (see page 49). On this page are the basic trimmings that will be most often used by the upholsterer, but if you wish to be more creative (particularly with cushions) there is a myriad of tassels, cords, and braids that you can buy from most fabric stores. Sometimes known as passementeries, there are also specialist stores (most of which can be found online) that carry enormous ranges of amazing trimmings.

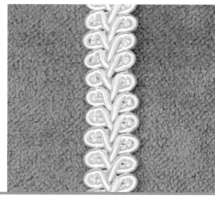

Piping (above), also known as welting, is the upholsterer's first choice of trimming because it is easy to make from fabric off-cuts and therefore comes free and matches the rest of the upholstery perfectly. Single piping is used on box cushions, seam edges, and scrolls, while double piping has the same applications as braid or gimp.

Gimp (above) is very similar in look to braid but is made to follow curves that braid cannot. It is mainly used to finish off the join where the fabric ends and the show wood begins.

Cord (above) is perennially popular and is available in a wide range of thicknesses, and plain or combination colors. Its flexibility and the fact that it gives the upholsterer the option of using a contrasting color to the upholstery fabric make it an ideal choice for outlining curved details, such as arm scrolls.

Braid (above) is a flat decorative band and is most suitable for straight lines, as it tends to ride up on curves. For this reason, it is mostly used to cover up staple and tack heads at the bottom of furniture. There are a vast array of colors, patterns, and styles available at an equally vast array of prices.

CHAPTER IV

TOOLS AND TECHNIQUES

Upholstered furniture is roughly divided into two categories: traditional and modern. Traditionally upholstered furniture uses jute webbing, burlap, coil springs, and fiber or horsehair for its stuffing. Modern, factory-produced furniture uses rubber webbing, zigzag springs, pre-formed foam and other modern materials to pad it.

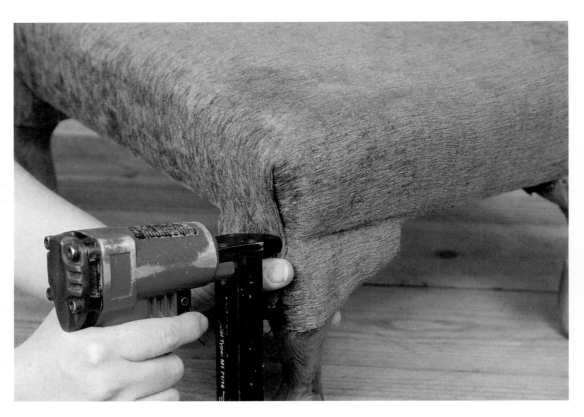

The options differ depending on what type of furniture you want to reupholster. Given the right knowledge and skill, there are few limitations to what you can do with a traditionally upholstered piece of furniture. You can completely strip back the furniture to the wood frame, repair it, and replace the old upholstery and springs so that it is as good as new. Your investment in time and money will be repaid by the increase in value of the old furniture.

Because of its construction and lack of intrinsic value, your options with modern furniture are more restricted. You can replace rubber webbing, zigzag springs and cushions, make slip covers or re-cover, but if the frame or foam padding has degraded to any extent, it would be better to buy new furniture than attempt to spend money on repair. Bear that in mind before you start stripping off old fabric or stuffing, and think about whether you are going to carefully replace the fabric on a modern sofa or completely take apart and renovate a hundred year old armchair.

UPHOLSTERY TOOLS

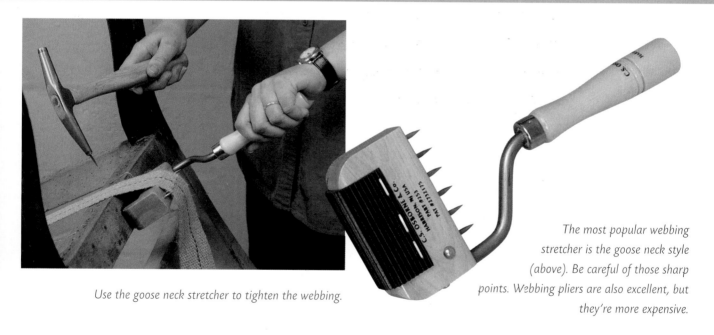

Use the goose neck stretcher to tighten the webbing.

The most popular webbing stretcher is the goose neck style (above). Be careful of those sharp points. Webbing pliers are also excellent, but they're more expensive.

A webbing stretcher increases the tension of the webbing in a seat base. Using this tool you can stretch the webbing tighter than you could manage using your hands alone. They come in various styles, but all use some method to grip the webbing and lever against the seat frame to achieve the required tension. Goose neck stretchers are the simplest to use, but the more expensive webbing pliers are also excellent.

TACK HAMMER

Tack hammers should be used in conjunction with upholstery tacks, and only on furniture with hardwood frames: in other words, traditionally upholstered furniture.

Unless you're going to use a staple gun, a magnetic tack hammer is essential for upholstery. It's like a normal tack hammer except that one end is magnetic so you can hold

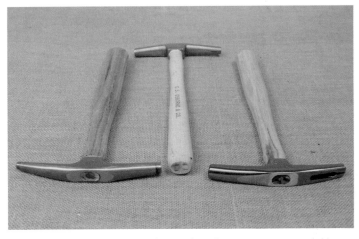

Top quality tack hammers are bronze, but cheaper ones are available.

tacks with it. If you sprinkle some tacks within reach on a plate, you can pick them up one at a time with the magnetic end, tack and hammer them home while holding the material in place with your free hand. You can buy expensive bronze-headed versions, but the cheaper ones work just as well.

MALLET

A wooden mallet is used to strike a tack, staple lifter, or ripping chisel to remove tacks and staples holding the old upholstery. Rubber mallets are also used by some upholsterers.

The two most popular mallets for upholsterers are the round-headed hickory (bottom) and the square beech (top).

STAPLE AND TACK LIFTERS

Staple and tack lifters are used to lever out loose tacks and staples, or in conjunction with a mallet to lever out firm ones. Generally a tack lifter will also remove staples, but a staple lifter, unsurprisingly, does it better.

From left to right: basic tack lifter, combined tack lifter and chisel, Berry staple lifter, Osbourne staple lifter.

STAPLE GUNS

Because of the widespread use of soft wood in the construction of modern furniture, staples should be used when reupholstering. Traditionally, upholstered furniture has frames made out of hardwood and so tacks can be used. But after many years and several re-coverings, staples are best used on those too. There are three types of staple guns used in upholstery: manual, electric, and pneumatic.

Manual staple gun

Electric staple gun

With manual staple guns, you squeeze a spring-loaded handle. This releases a driver that punches a staple out of the end of the gun.

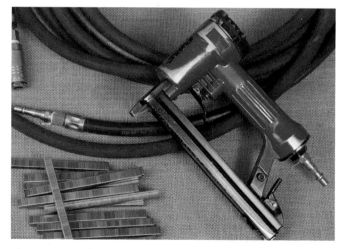

Pneumatic staple gun

Electric versions substitute hand strength for electro-magnets that fire the staple driver.

Pneumatic staple guns use compressed air that is generated by a compressor to fire the staple driver. They are more expensive than manual staple guns but less expensive than electric guns. Staple guns use compressed air at a pressure of around 45lbs, so you don't need a large or expensive compressor. However, compressors of any size are noisy when reaching and maintaining constant pressure. Silent versions are very expensive.

An electric staple gun is probably the best choice for the DIY upholsterer. If you are really keen and intend to upholster lots of things over a long period of time, invest in a pneumatic gun and small compressor.

NEEDLES

Five regulators are shown (center): four in various lengths with plastic handles and one without a handle. A double ended needle is seen (bottom) and to the left is a curved needle.

For upholstery you can use the the double-ended needle stitch with various upholstery twines. The double-ended needle is used for stitching fox edges (edges mounted over spring edges around the outside edge of seats, usually with coil springs), through stuffing ties, and for buttoning.

Regulators are strong thick needles, like knitting needles, with a flat end or plastic handle. When you cover fiber or horsehair stuffing with burlap or muslin (see the Dining Chair with Drop Seat, page 66), the stuffing needs to be distributed more evenly, moved up to make a firmer edge, or pushed into corners. This is done by using a regulator to lever the fiber inside the pad to wherever you want it.

In addition to the specialist tools mentioned above, you will also need a pair of scissors, tape measure, pliers, knife, and needles for hand stitching.

KNIFE

You don't have to buy special upholstery scissors and a knife, but a good pair of scissors is invaluable when cutting large amounts of fabric, and upholstery knives are specifically designed for stripping furniture.

You can buy a knife specially made for upholstery like the one shown here.

SEWING MACHINE

A sewing machine is essential for making welting and cushions. A good quality home sewing machine that can be used for dressmaking and curtains is fine for most upholstery applications. Obviously, if you're going to want to work with leather or other tough materials, you'll need to get a machine that can cope with such tasks—ideally an industrial one. You can make welting and stitch in zippers with an ordinary zipper foot, but a double welting foot is needed if you want to make double welting.

A good quality sewing machine is suitable for most upholstery.

STRIPPING FURNITURE

The object of the stripping process is to remove all the upholstery so that you can repair or re-cover it. The last thing you put on a sofa or chair is the bottom cloth or dust cover, and stripping the old fabric and upholstery off is the reverse of this, so start with the underside. Turn the piece over so that you are looking at the bottom cloth, if it has one, and using a tack/staple lifter, start removing the tacks or staples holding it on.

Loose tacks or staples can be levered out by hand. Remove firm tacks by holding the tack lifter up against the tack head and hammering with a mallet, while levering upwards. Once the bottom cloth is off you'll have access to the staples or tacks securing the webbing, and top fabric, and burlap underneath. Use scissors or a knife to cut stitches and pliers to remove stubborn tacks and staples.

Keep going until you have removed all you need to make your repair, but no more than you have to.

Hold the tack lifter against the tack and hammer it with a mallet, while levering upwards.

You can also use pliers to remove lose staples.

FRAME REPAIRING TIPS

It's important to give the piece you want to upholster a good checking over before you do anything. Most important is that you check out, as best you can, the condition of the frame. Unless you intend to remove all the upholstery, the frame will be mostly inaccessible, so you won't be able to make good any repairs.

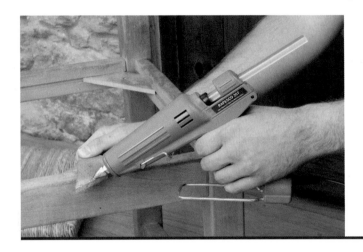

You can make minor repairs using a glue gun.

If you see evidence of insect damage you will need to treat the whole frame, repairing any weakened joints.

If a traditionally upholstered chair is in generally good condition but feels a little wobbly in the frame, have a look underneath at the jute webbing. Webbing is supposed to be under tension to form a firm base and pull the frame together. If old webbing is loose and rotten, replacing it with tight, new webbing will make a big difference to the stability of the frame. However, if the chair has had a great deal of use while in a poor condition, all the frame's joints will probably be loose and possibly broken. This is particularly true of chairs or sofas that have been used when one of the castors has fallen off and the frame has been twisted as a result.

Upholstery, particularly in traditionally upholstered furniture, plays a big part in holding the frame together. Major damage to the frame and its joints may only show up as slight instability in the chair until all the upholstery is removed. If you have any doubts about a frame's integrity, you should either be prepared to strip all the upholstery off and repair the frame properly, or find another project. This is particularly true of insect damage. If you can see evidence of it, such as fine wood dust trapped under the upholstery, an appropriate pesticide treatment will successfully treat the parts of the frame that you can apply it to. But often insects will attack the soft wood dowels that form the joints deep inside the chair and leave the frame weak. Again, unless you're prepared to expose all the frame, find another chair.

REPAIRING OR REPLACING JUTE WEBBING

You'll find jute webbing is the supporting platform of all traditional upholstery. Not only does it form a firm, elastic foundation for springs, stuffing, and all the upholstery that goes on top, but it also pulls the wood frame together so that it becomes a strong, weight bearing structure. It's up to you whether to replace or repair jute webbing, but the webbed base of your project chair or sofa must be made strong before you go on to do any other repair work on the upholstery.

If you're going to replace the webbing, remove all the tacks or staples attaching it to the wooden frame. If there are coil springs, cut through the stitches holding them to the webbing. Reweb the base as shown below and stitch the springs back on to the new webbing so that the springs don't move.

If you're going to repair the webbing, leave the old webbing in place so that the coil springs are held firm, and reinforce it with new webbing over the top.

The process of applying webbing to the seat base is the same whether you're repairing or replacing the old webbing: Attach one end of the webbing to one side of the seat frame and run it across to the opposite side. Apply tension to the webbing using a webbing stretcher and hold it while you attach the other end of the webbing to the seat frame.

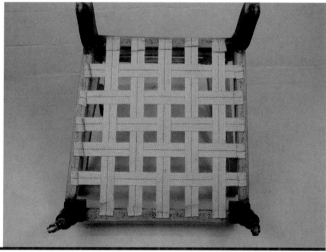

1 Once you've attached all the webbing running from one side to the other, repeat with the webbing on the other two opposite sides, weaving in and out alternately as you go.

2 Each end of the webbing is attached using tacks or staples. If you're using tacks, make sure you use proper upholstery tacks: $5/8$ inch is long enough. Don't use nails as these will cause damage to the frame.

REATTACHING SPRINGS AND COILS

If you need to reattach coil springs to a webbed base, use a curved spring needle and strong twine. Start off by tying a slip knot in the end of your twine and stitch over the base of each spring in four places. Move on to the next in turn until all the springs are in place. Make sure the twine is pulled tight through all the stitches and then tie off.

Stitch over the base of each spring in four places

TYING AN UPHOLSTERER'S SLIP KNOT

The only knot you have to know how to tie for most upholstery purposes is the upholsterer's slip knot. It's used extensively for tufting and starting most stitching operations where twine or other thicker thread is used. Here's how to tie it.

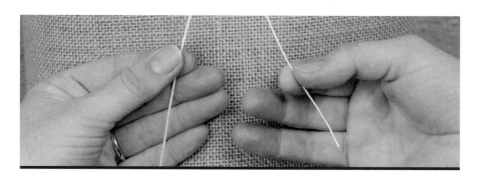

1   Take the short end of a length of twine in one hand.

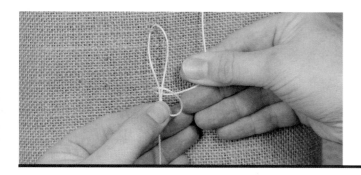

2   Hold the middle of the two lengths between the thumb and finger of your other hand, and with the first hand, wrap the short end around the two lengths, leaving a loop.

3   Wrap the short end around two more times and then thread it through the loop. Pull the knot tight and the slip knot should slip up and down the long end of the twine.

REPLACING PADDING AND OR STUFFING

DIY upholsterers should restrict themselves to recovering modern upholstered furniture or carrying out minor repairs, such as replacing webbing, and recovering traditionally upholstered furniture. To be able to fully reupholster a traditionally upholstered piece of furniture takes many hours of study and dedication, and replacing the foam padding on a modern piece is probably not economically viable.

So think carefully before you embark on any major replacement of padding or stuffing. Check out the condition of the upholstery on the seat particularly, as this is the weight bearing part of the furniture and where most degradation is likely to be. Other places to check are the tops of the arms and back.

If you do need to replace any stuffing, carefully remove the old degraded parts such as batting and crumbled foam and replace with new. Foam sheets of varying density and thickness are commonly available and most suppliers will offer a cut to size service.

On old upholstery, add to what's there rather than remove. Apply a new layer of burlap or muslin for strength, and reapply a new layer of batting. Always put a layer of thin Dacron over as a last layer before you apply the top fabric, as this will allow the fabric to slide over the upholstery and prevent it from breaking up the batting during the re-covering and also when the chair is back in use.

CUTTING AND FITTING THE FABRIC

For most DIY upholstery projects, the primary concern will be how much fabric to buy. Even if you have a good general experience with estimating yardage, you would be best advised to carefully and systematically measure the sofa or chair and put together a cutting plan. It may seem daunting and laborious compared with just using guesswork, but fabric will be the main and major expense of reupholstering.

Overestimating will cause unnecessary expense and even worse, underestimating might prove disastrous should you not be able to get more of the same fabric.

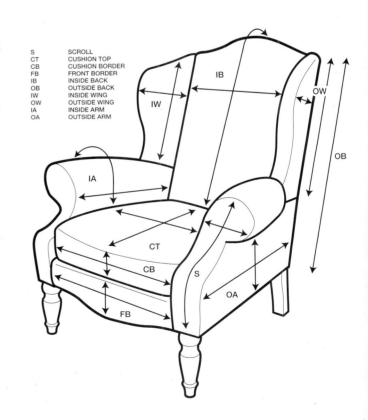

S	SCROLL
CT	CUSHION TOP
CB	CUSHION BORDER
FB	FRONT BORDER
IB	INSIDE BACK
OB	OUTSIDE BACK
IW	INSIDE WING
OW	OUTSIDE WING
IA	INSIDE ARM
OA	OUTSIDE ARM

The diagram of a wing chair (below left) shows where to take measurements for the table and cutting plan that you will prepare. Make sure when you take the measurements to use a flexible tape measure and that you push the measure down into the edges of the deck when measuring the inside back and arms, and add 5 or 6 inches for safety.

On a piece of paper, make three columns (like the table shown right). In the first, write the name or initials representing the measurement taken. In the second, write the measurement from top to bottom. In the third, write the measurement from side to side.

On another piece of paper, preferably graph paper, draw a diagrammatical representation of a length of fabric rolled out on the floor. Most rolls of fabric are around 54 inches wide, but check with

Wing Chair Measurements Table

Area to be covered	Height (in.)	Width (in.)
inside back	38	22
outside back	39	26
inside arm	28	35
	28	33
outside arm	15	31
	15	31
inside wing	24	16
	24	16
seat/deck	22	35
front border	15	27
scroll	24	9
	25	9
cushion:		
top	25	23
bottom	25	23
front boxing	4	23
side boxing	22	4
	22	4
back boxing	5	27
welting		10 yards

your supplier and write this measurement along the top of the cutting plan. Using the width measurement, fit the rectangular pieces of fabric from the measurements table onto the imaginary roll of fabric in the most economical way you can. Keep going, adding yards to your cutting plan, until all the pieces are accounted for. Use spare areas for welting, scrolls etc. Add half a yard for safety and if you intend to use a fabric with a large pattern, as a very rough guide, add another half a yard so that you can match it up. More accurately, yardage must be adjusted according to the pattern repeats. For example, if

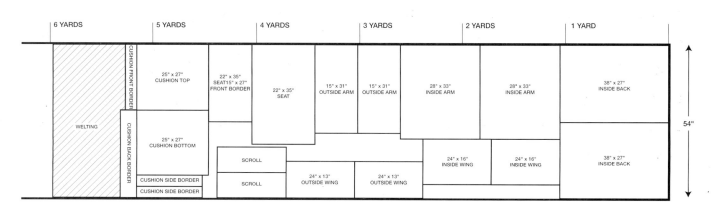

the cut is 35 inches and the pattern is a 20-inch repeat, then the necessary length becomes 55 inches if you have to match, say, across a back or on cushions.

FILLING SCROLLS/ROLLED ARMS

Rolled arms are finished at the front with a scroll shape. The scroll can be filled in many ways but here's how to give them the professional look

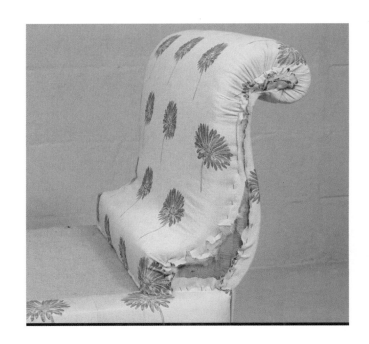

1   Trim off all the excess fabric around the front of the scroll.

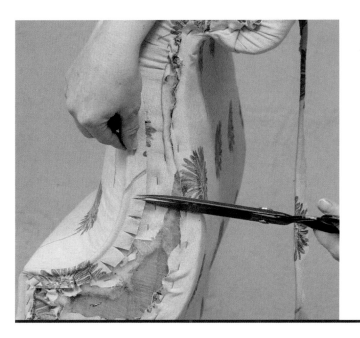

2   Make up a length of welting and start attaching it around the outside of the scroll making small cuts into the welt so that it follows the curve of the scroll.

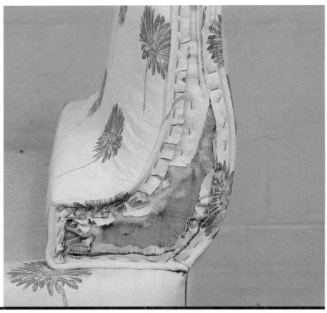

3   Make sure you join the welting in a place where it's not going to be noticed so that the line around the scroll looks continuous.

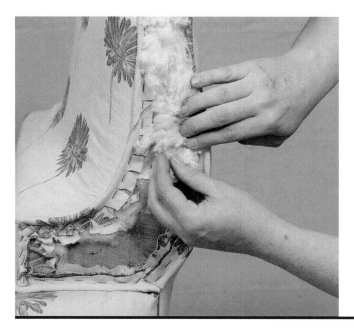

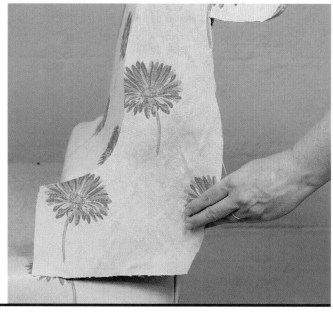

4 Tease some batting apart and carefully fill the area inside the welting.

5 Cut out a piece of fabric the same shape, but larger than the area inside the welting border.

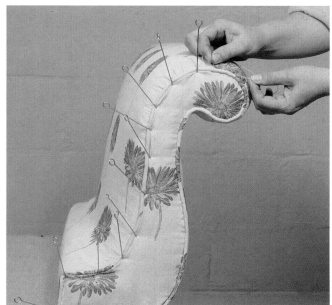

6 Carefully, and making small cuts where necessary to follow the curve of the scroll, fold the edges of the fabric under and use skewers to hold them in place until the whole of the area inside the welting border is filled with fabric.

7 Finally, go around the whole scroll, hand-stitching the scroll fabric to the welting and the welting to the arm fabric.

TUFTING (BUTTONING)

Tufting adds a professional touch to any upholstery, and it's really not that difficult to do, especially when recovering a modern piece with a preformed foam back. Carefully remove the old fabric and use it as a template for marking out the button positions on the new fabric.

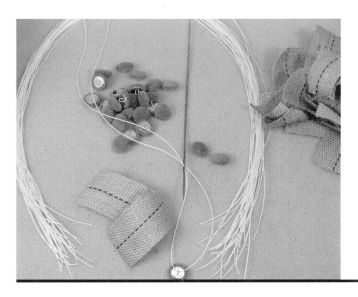

1 To button your top fabric, you'll need some buttons covered in the same fabric, lengths of buttoning twine, small pieces of webbing or other strong material, and a long double-ended needle.

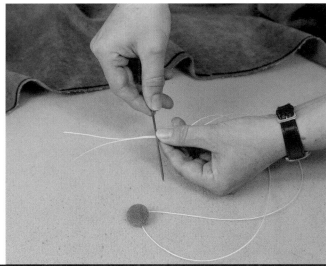

2 Thread the button loop with one end of the twine and pass both ends of the twine through the double-ended needle.

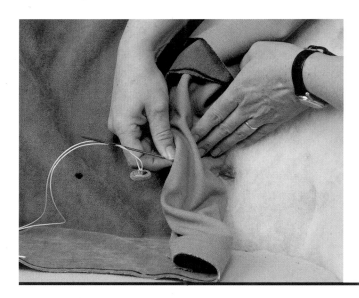

3 Pass the unthreaded end of the needle through your fabric where the button is meant to go, and through the center of the button hole in your upholstery.

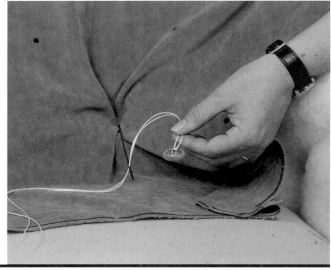

4 Push the needle all the way in until it reaches the other side of the upholstery. Reach around the back and pull it through so that the buttoning twine follows it through the fabric, button hole, and out the other side.

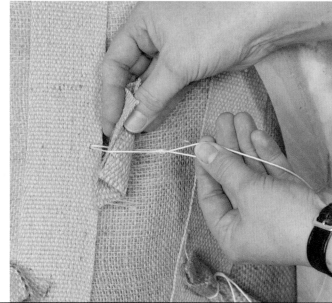

5 Where they've passed out the back, take hold of both ends of the twine and tie a slip knot.

6 Slip a folded piece of webbing or other strong material in between the lengths of twine in front of the slip knot.

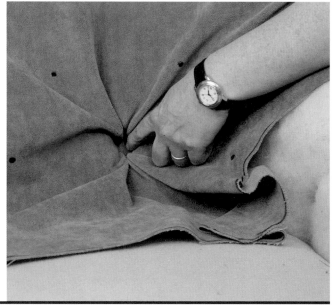

7 Pull the slip knot tight up against the webbing piece so that it pulls the button into the button hole in the upholstery.

8 Finally make sure the button is pushed down in position in the upholstery before moving on to the next button.

HAND STITCHING

When hand-stitching a fabric seam, or piping to fabric, use a curved needle, a strong thread, and ladder stitch the seam together:

1 Stitch one side of the seam.

2 Pull the thread through.

3 Enter the other side of the seam exactly opposite where the needle exited.

4 Keep the tension in the thread and continue stitching. The seams will be invisibly pulled together without puckering.

MAKING SINGLE PIPING

Piping is used for, among other things, cushions, scrolls, and finishing edges, and double piping can be used to finish off edges as an alternative to decorative braid or gimp. To make piping you need fabric, piping cord, and a sewing machine with a zipper foot.

1   Lay a piece of fabric out, take one corner, fold it over to the opposite side, and cut along the diagonal. Using the diagonal as your guide, cut strips of fabric two or three inches wide until you have sufficient strips for the required length of piping.

2   Trim the ends of the fabric strips so they all have the same angle, and lay two pieces end to end on the sewing machine so their angles correspond. Take one end and turn it over so that the two pieces form a right angle and, using an ordinary stitching foot, stitch the ends together half an inch in from the edge of the fabric.

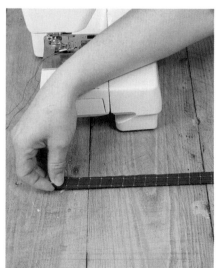

3   Do this with all the strips and straighten them out into one long strip. Flatten out the joins and place the piping cord over the top.

4   Use a zipper or double piping foot. Fold the fabric over the cord. If using a zipper foot, drop and rest it against the cord.

5   Stitch and fold the fabric over the cord as you go. Make sure you flatten out joins in the fabric before you stitch over them.

MITERING CORNERS

Fabric corners can be finished off in many ways, but one of the most often used is a method called mitering, or pleating. You can do a single miter or a double, but basically it's a way of neatly folding the fabric at the front corner of a chair or sofa so that it looks clean and well finished—a bit like gift wrapping. A double miter is called a kiss pleat. Here's how you do both:

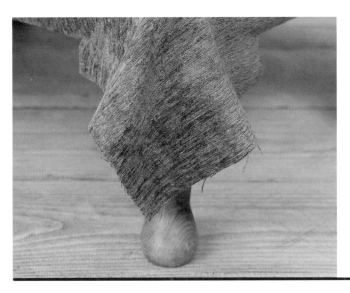

1 *Single Miter* Start with the corner fabric hanging over the leg of the chair, after it's been attached underneath the deck up to the point where it meets the leg. Sometimes you'll want to finish it with a double miter, but this one is going to be finished with a single miter.

2 Pull the front-facing fabric tight up to the corner and staple it along the top of the leg, but only on the front-facing side.

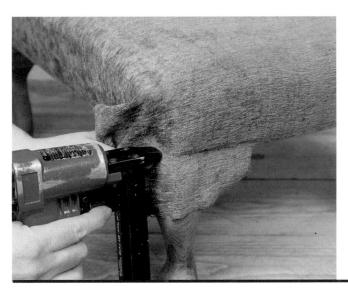

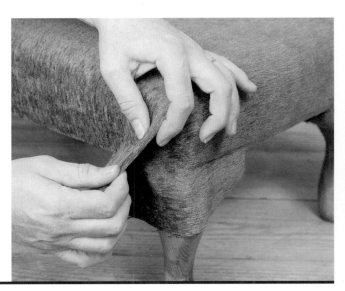

3 Pull the front-facing fabric tight around the corner and staple it once along the top of the leg on the other side of the corner.

4 Form a fold in the fabric on the side-facing fabric so that the fold runs vertically down, or slightly to the side of the center of the corner.

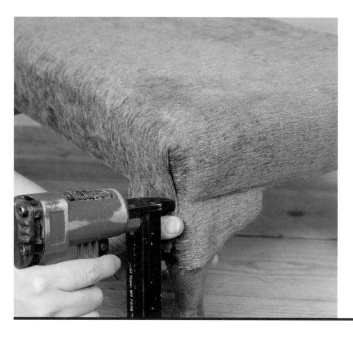

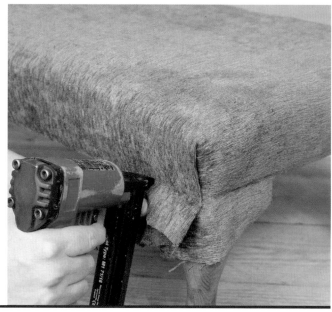

5 Hold the fold tight and staple it in position, where the fabric meets the top of the leg.

6 Carry on stapling along the top of the leg moving away from the corner, until you get to where the fabric is tucked underneath the deck ra l.

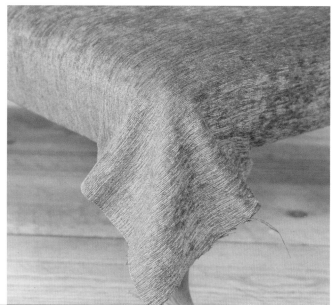

7 Use a sharp knife or scissors to trim the excess fabric away from the top of the leg.

1 *Double Miter* To make a double miter, start at exactly the same point in the seat covering process as in Step 1 on page 50.

2 Pull the excess corner fabric straight down and feel for the apex of the corner with your fingers. Keep the fabric tight, smoothing it out evenly away to each side of the corner.

3 Hold the fabric tight and staple it in place at the front near the apex of the corner, doing the same on the other side of the corner.

4 Form a fold with the loose fabric and bring it into the point of the corner at a slight angle. Hold the fold and staple in place just above the wood of the leg.

5 Form a fold which mirrors the fold on the other side and staple it in place as before.

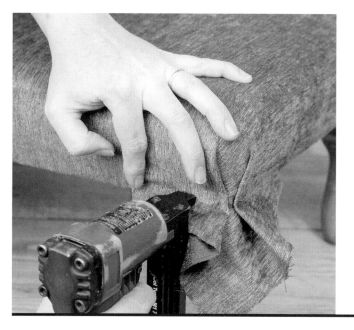

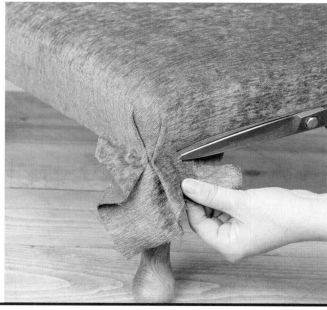

6 Staple back from the corner along the line of the leg wood on both sides until you reach the point where the fabric turns under the deck rail.

7 Trim off the excess fabric along the top of the leg with a sharp pair of scissors or a knife.

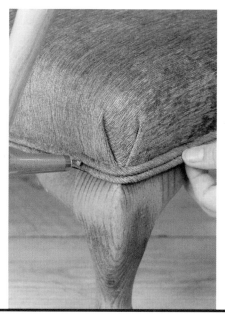

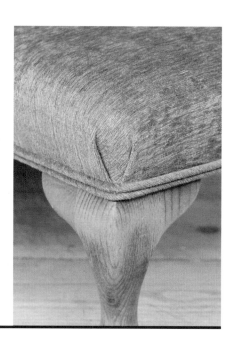

8 Once the fabric is trimmed off, the heads of the staples or tacks need to be hidden under braid, gimp, or some other form of trimming.

9 Here we finish off the corner with a length of double piping held in place with blue gimp pins. Hot glue guns are also excellent for invisibly attaching trimmings.

10 The end result is a neat professional finish to a double miter corner, or kiss pleat.

MAKING A BOLSTER CUSHION OR PILLOW

Box cushions and T-cushions of whatever shape and size are made in exactly the same manner. To get the cushion to fit the exact shape required, use a paper template laid over the seat where the cushion is to fit, draw out the exact shape on the paper, cut it out, and transfer it to the fabric. Remember to allow for seam widths.

Making round bolster cushions (like the ones seen in the Upholstered Sofa with Serpentine Arms project on page 74) has to be approached in a different manner. Here's how you make them:

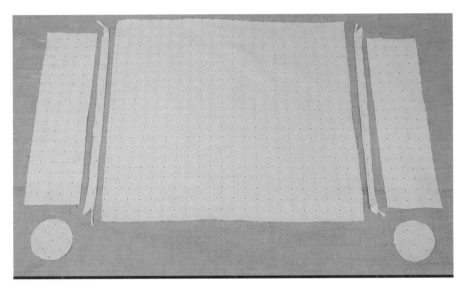

1 A bolster cushion comprises two ends, two lengths of piping, a center piece, and two finishing discs.

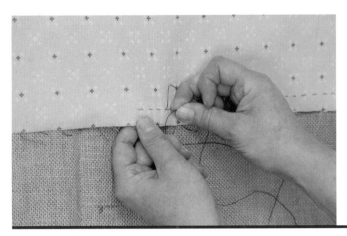

2 Take the center piece and, making sure that the first stitch is tied so it won't slip, put a line of running stitches all along from top to bottom, a half inch or so in from the edge. Do this to both ends.

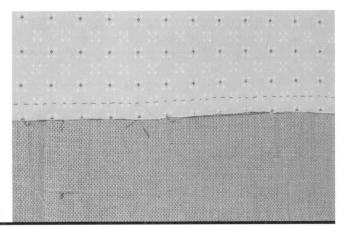

3 This is what each end should look like with the running stitches in place. Leave the last stitch loose with the thread hanging.

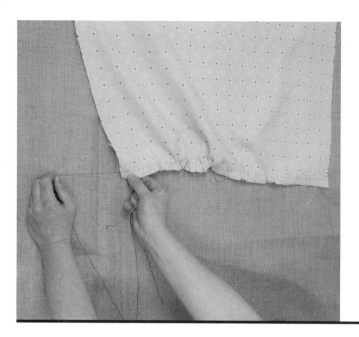

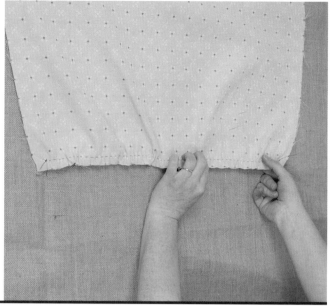

4 Hold the loose thread tight and slide the edge of the fabric up so that the stitches start to bunch until the edge is about one fifth reduced in length. Knot the last stitch so it can't slip back, then repeat with the other end.

5 Even up the bunching along the whole length of the side.

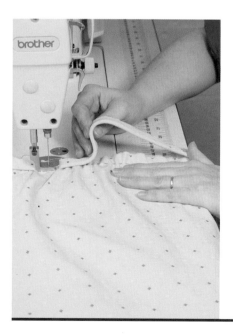

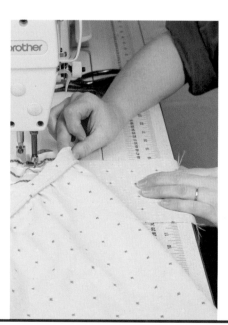

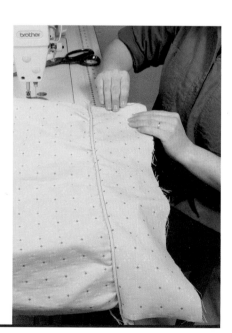

6 Transfer the center piece to a sewing machine and stitch the two lengths of piping over the top of the bunched ends.

7 Turn the center piece over and lie it on top of one of the end pieces, so that they are face to face. Stitch the piped edge to the long edge of the end piece.

8 When finished, each end should now look like this, with the center piece one side of the piping and the end piece the other.

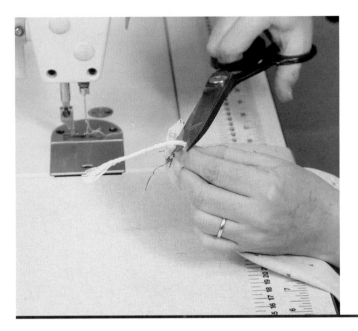

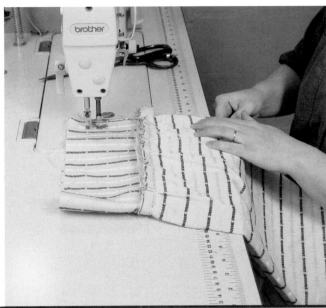

9 Carefully snip off the excess piping cord at each end, so that when the open fabric forms a tube, the piping will join neatly without any bulky overlap.

10 Take the center piece with the end pieces attached, fold it in half lengthways, and stitch along the open side half an inch in from the edge.

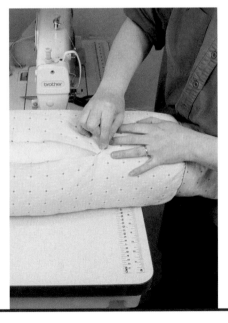

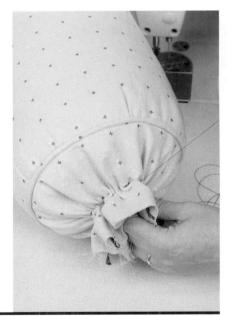

11 Make sure you leave a gap in the center of the bolster cover to help when filling it with whatever stuffing you choose.

12 Stuff the middle of the bolster cover and slip stitch the hole in the seam closed.

13 Gather up the fabric at each end of the bolster and sew a running stitch around where it meets in the center, so that you can pull it up tight.

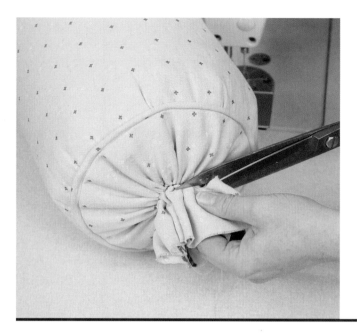

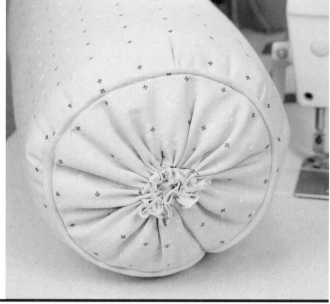

14 Tie the running stitch off so it won't come loose, and trim off the excess fabric from the ends.

15 After trimming off the excess fabric, the bolster is almost done. All that s needed to finish is to cover the fabric ends.

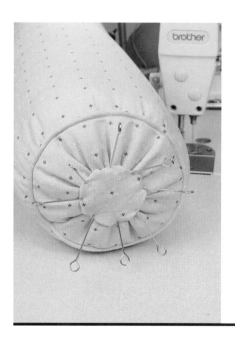

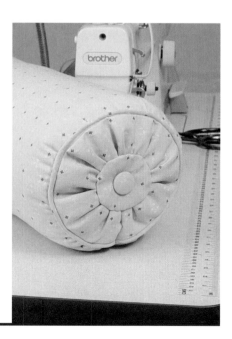

16 Take a disk of fabric and skewer it in place over the fabric ends, with the edges turned under.

17 The finishing disk of fabric is slip-stitched in place.

18 Bolster cushions are quite a flamboyant addition to a piece of furniture, so they can always benefit from more trimming, such as a tassel. This one was finished with a button.

MAKING BOX CUSHIONS

Box cushions can be filled with any number of loose or solid fillings to suit their requirements. Solid fillers like foam should be covered in Dacron, so that they don't chafe the outer cover. Loose fillings should be contained in an inner cushion cover to stop them from escaping. If using down, the inner cover must be made of a feather-proof material such as glazed cambric or ticking. Outer cushion covers should be made to the exact size and shape required by using the old fabric or paper as a template. Incorporate a long zipper around the back end, so that the filling can easily be removed and the cover washed.

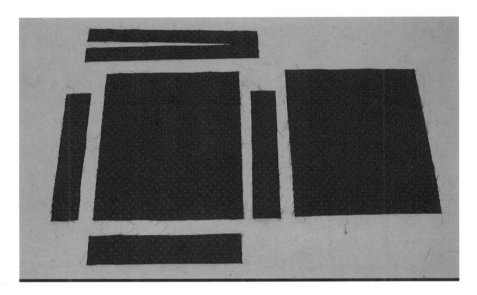

1 For a basic rectangular box cushion you will need to cut out a top, a bottom, a front, two sides, and two pieces to go around the zipper. Make enough welting to go around the top and bottom.

2 Sew the welting around the edges of the top and bottom pieces, making cuts into the flange of the welting to allow it to go smoothly around the corners.

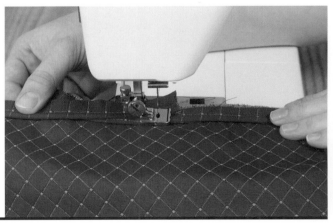

3 Make a smooth join between the ends of the welting by cutting back the cord from both sides and sewing across the two pieces.

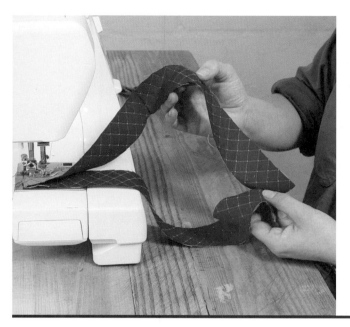

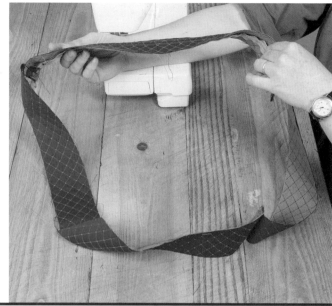

4 Sew the first inch of each end of the zipper pieces together and then insert your zipper.

5 Sew the front sides and zipper pieces together to form the cushion border.

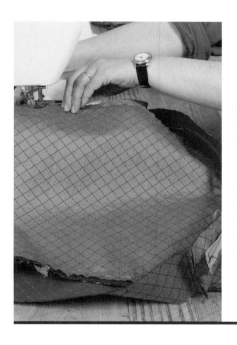

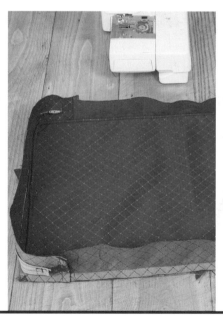

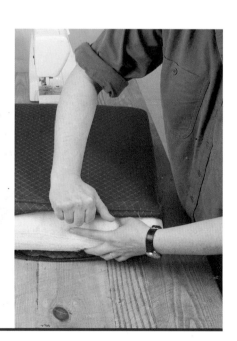

6 Place the outside faces of the fabric together and sew the border to the cushion top. Use a zipper foot on your sewing machine and sew tight up to the welting.

7 Before you start to sew the bottom piece on to the top piece and border, make sure you open the zipper so that you can turn the cover out the right way when you have finished.

8 Getting the inner cushion into the cover will be made a lot easier if you have extended the zipper a couple of inches around the sides.

UPHOLSTERED ARMLESS DINING CHAIR

Before

Upholstered dining chairs that don't have drop-in seats are an excellent first project for the novice upholsterer. The simplicity of the design means that the fabric goes all the way over the frame and attaches underneath. Re-covering a chair like the modern chair here is very straightforward and well within the capabilities of the most ungifted of do-it-yourselfers.

After

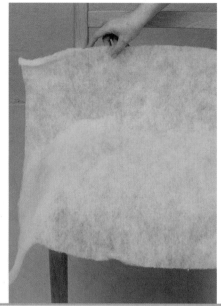

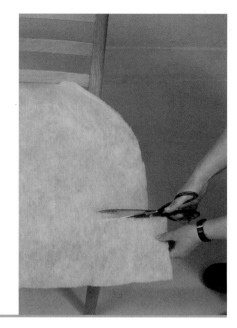

1 Measure the area and, ensuring that you make allowances for tucking under, cut out the fabric.

2 Take a piece of Dacron and lay it over the chair seat.

3 Carefully cut right angles into the Dacron so that it will fit around the front legs.

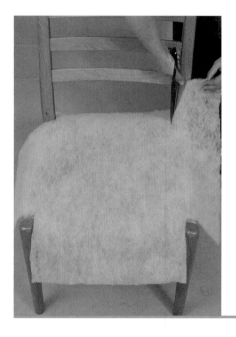

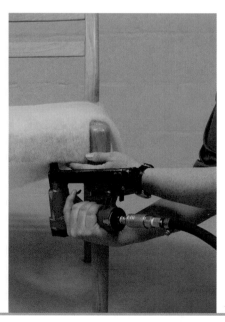

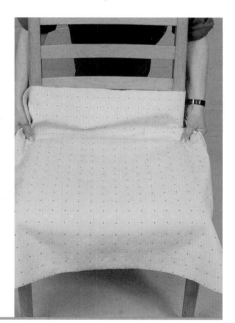

4 Do the same at the back, so that it will fit around the back supports.

5 Staple the Dacron in place all around the underside of the chair.

6 Lay your piece of fabric over the seat and ensure that the pattern is level and up the right way. If there is a nap, for example if you're using velvet or chenile, make sure that it runs from back to front.

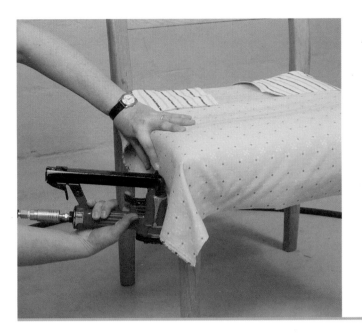

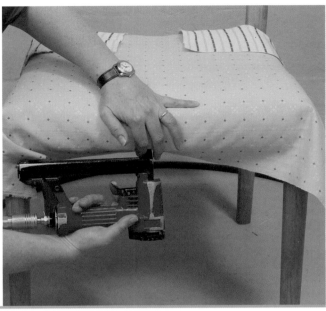

7 Lift the back corners up so that they lie over the seat where the back rests are. Start to staple the fabric in place.

8 Staple systematically, alternating from front to back and side to side.

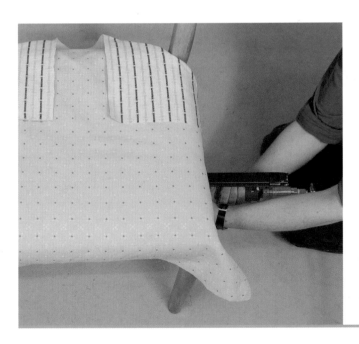

9 Start stapling in the middle of each side and work your way out towards the corners.

10 Finish the back corners around the back rests by cutting straight into the back rest at a 45-degree angle.

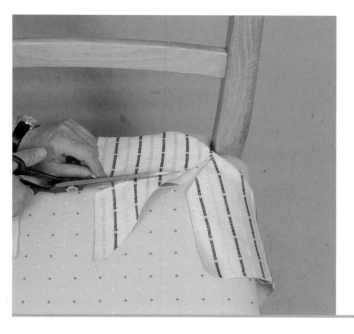

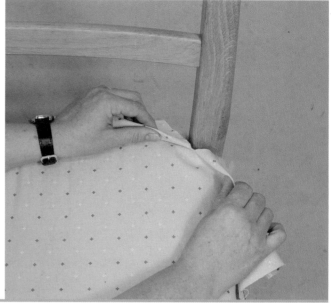

11 Trim off the excess, so that when you fold the fabric it doesn't become too bulky.

12 Fold the fabric under either side of the cut and take it towards the back rest.

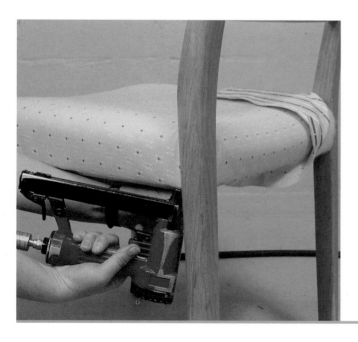

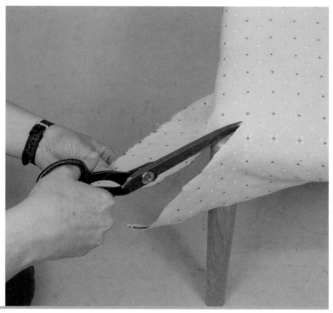

13 Pull the sides of the fabric to either side of the back rest. Make sure you form a neat fold tight up against each side of the back rest before taking the fabric underneath the seat and stapling it in place.

14 Finish the front corners in a similar fashion by taking the excess fabric and cutting into it at a 45-degree angle up to the back corner of the chair leg. Go carefully with the cut; the only thing you can do wrong is cut too far.

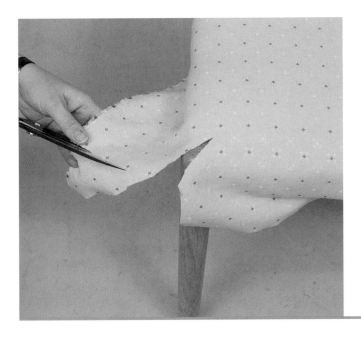

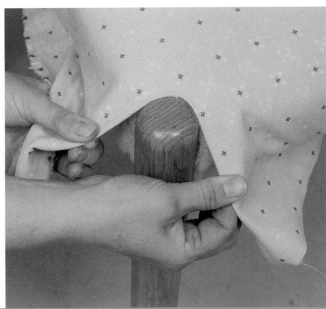

15 Cut off the excess fabric so as to not make the corner folds too bulky.

16 Fold the two sides of the cut under and take them out to each side of the chair leg.

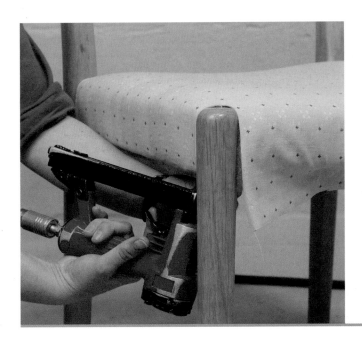

17 Pull the sides of the fabric to either side of the front leg. Make sure you form a neat fold tight up against each side before taking the fabric underneath the seat and stapling it in place.

18 Staple the fabric in place up tight to the chair legs on both sides.

19 As long as you didn't cut too far into the front corners, the chair should look as if it's just come out of the shop.

DINING CHAIR WITH DROP SEAT

Before

The drop-in bottom seat is a separate removable seat frame, upholstered and fitted within the seat rails. It is found mainly in dining chairs, but also in piano stools and the like. The chair in this project is probably 100 years old, so it's going to be upholstered traditionally using natural fiber stuffing. If the chair was more modern and contained foam stuffing the procedure would be the same but a shaped piece of foam would be substituted for the fiber.

After

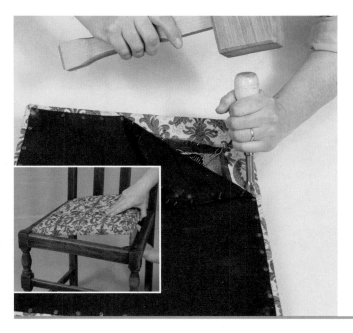

1 Remove the seat pad from the chair and strip all the old upholstery from it. Take a good look at the frame and see if it needs any repairs. Don't be overly concerned about tack holes, but if it's been upholstered many times you may want to squirt some wood glue into the worst of them and leave it to dry before carrying on.

2 It's a good idea to fit the bare frame back into the chair to see how it fits and how much gap there is around the edges of the frame. Bear in mind that your chosen fabric is going to have to fit in whatever gap there is, so if it's a tight fit you may have to change your mind about having thick, heavy fabric.

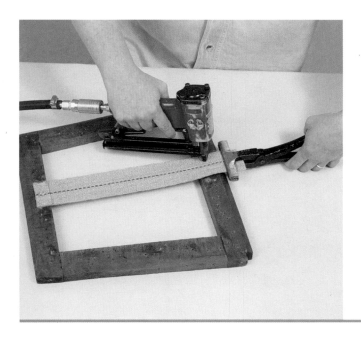

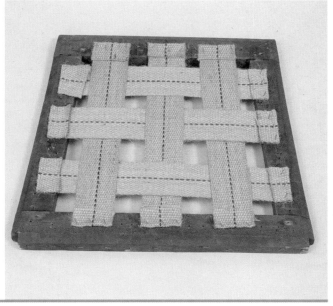

3 Re-web the seat, leaving a clear gap between the end of the webbing and the edge of the seat frame. Don't overtighten webbing on a drop-in bottom seat as its frame isn't as strong as normal chair frames and can break.

4 Weave the webbing from side to side, under and over the strips running from top to bottom, so that it forms a firm, self-supporting base for the pad.

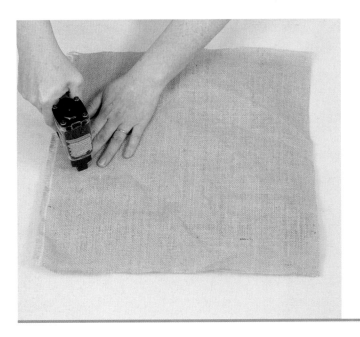

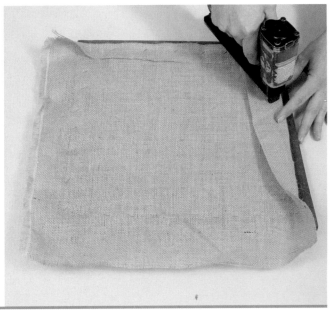

5 Cut a piece of burlap large enough to cover the whole of the seat pad with at least a 1-inch overlap. Lay it over the webbed frame and staple it down. There's no need to apply tension, just pull the wrinkles out as you go.

6 Fold the edges over and tack them down. Make sure that you leave at least $\frac{1}{2}$ inch of clear wood around the frame so that the chamfered, or rounded-off, edge is uncovered.

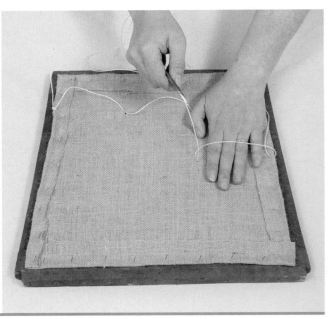

7 Trim off the excess burlap. Because the seat pad is a small area, it's important to leave yourself as much room as possible in the early stages, so that you don't run out of room for upholstery in the later stages. If you're going to use foam for a stuffing go to Step 11.

8 Stitch some stuffing ties to the surface of the burlap (wide stitches of twine to hold stuffing in place). Tie a slip knot to one end of a length of twine. Take a spring needle, stitch through the burlap on the edge about 4 inches from the top, then pass the twine through the slip knot and pull tight. Use your hand as a guide to loop size.

9 Move down about 4 inches and stitch back to the edge you started from. Continue stitching the rows of loops until the surface of the burlap is covered. Take a handful of fiber, discard any lumps, tease it into a ball, and slip it under one of the stuffing ties. Carry on until the seat frame is evenly covered.

10 How much fiber to use and how tightly to pack it is something you learn by trial and error. When you first start it's natural to underestimate, so use more than you think. The fiber will pack down and you want a firm pad, so squash it down with your hands and imagine the sort of seat it will make.

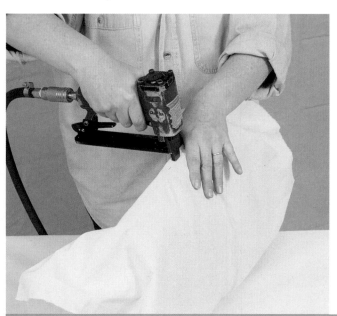

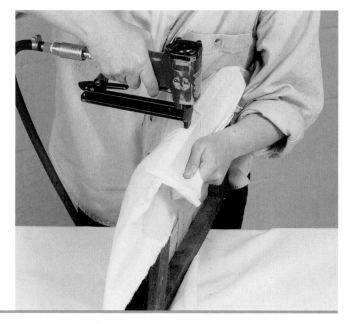

11 When you're happy with the stuffing, cut a piece of muslin to fit over it. You will need enough left over to grip and pull, so be generous. Lay the muslin over the pad and staple the middle of one side to the edge of the frame.

12 Using the heal of your hand, smooth and stretch the muslin from one side to the other and staple it in place.

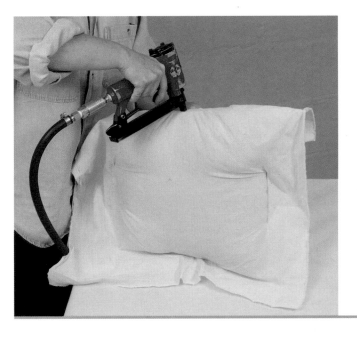

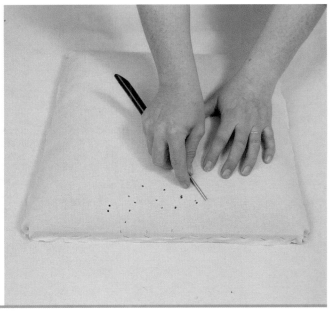

13 Continue adding staples, working your way out from the middle of each side towards the corners. Make sure you keep stretching the muslin, so the fiber or foam is pulled down into a shapely pad.

14 The compacted fiber within the muslin will need to be regulated to get rid of any lumps and bumps. You will need to force it into all the corners and edges until the pad feels even and the shape looks regular. Take your regulator, push it into the fiber, and lever the fiber where you want it to go. Feel for lumps with your free hand and concentrate your effort around the edges.

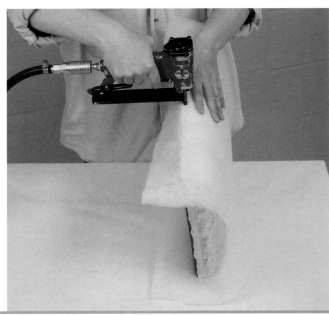

15 Cut out a piece of batting to fit over the top of the pad and then tease away the sides to shape, so that it fits over exactly and the sides are thinned out.

16 Batting breaks up very easily, so cover it with a layer of Dacron to hold it in place and protect it. It isn't essential, but it does make working on top of the batting much easier.

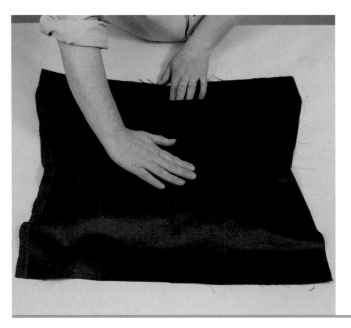

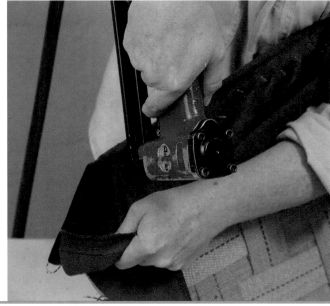

17 Cut out sufficient fabric to fit over the seat pad and fold underneath. Spend time lining up the fabric on the seat ensuring that it's symmetrical, that any prominent feature of the pattern is in the right place, and that it's up the right way. Or, if using a fabric with a nap, like velvet, make sure the nap runs from back to front.

18 Fold the fabric under the edges of the seat pad and staple it in place. Start in the middle of the front, then back and side to side, smoothing as you go. Turn it over and check that the fabric is still positioned correctly before you go too far, just in case you need to realign it.

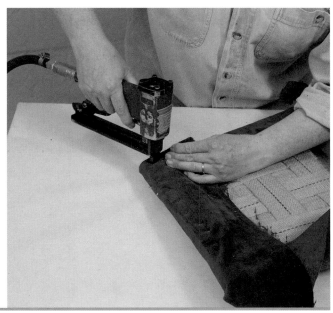

19 To finish the corners, pull the fabric back over the corner so that it forms a sharp tight fold on the front facing edge.

20 Pull the fabric tight under the frame and staple it in place. Turn the pad around and do the other front corner, then the back corners. Ensure that you make all the corner folds so that they lie on the front and rear facing edges of the seat pad and not the sides.

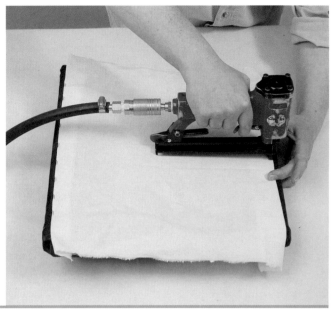

21   The corners are particularly important in a drop-in seat project, because if they're too bulky the seat won't fit back into the chair frame. The secret is to make a few practice folds and as long as you keep the fabric tight and the folds sharp, the result will be neat and inconspicuous and fit into the frame.

22   The last job after trimming off any excess fabric is to fit a bottom cloth. A piece of muslin was used on this small job. Woven or non-woven cambric is is also a good choice for smaller jobs. It is a strong, yet workable, dustproof fabric.

23   The end result should look neat and tidy to give the chair a professional finish.

24   Finally, slot the seat back into the frame and it will look as good as new.

25 If the chair is part of a set of chairs, make sure you buy enough material to re-cover all of them. Re-covering a chair such as this adds a lot more value than the cost of materials and is well worth the effort.

UPHOLSTERED SOFA WITH SERPENTINE ARMS AND BOLSTER CUSHIONS

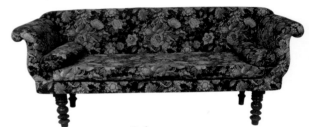

Before

The upholstered settle (i.e. unsprung) sofa in this project is a good example of an alternative method of furniture construction common to many traditionally upholstered sofas. Reupholstery of this type of sofa is much easier because the deck and back are separate pieces that are screwed together. Once you gain access to the screws holding the two together, the back can be removed and both pieces reupholstered separately, which is a great benefit. This sofa has a firm, wooden bench-style deck with a thin box cushion and serpentine arms that accommodate round cushions, known as bolsters.

After

1   Take time (before you start taking anything apart) to assess the sofa and visualize how you
    are going to approach reupholstery. Think about any potential problems the sofa will
    present. One potential problem with this particular sofa is that it is 7 feet wide. With a sofa
    this size a roll of fabric isn't wide enough to cover the back and deck cushion in one piece.
    One or more pieces of fabric will have to be joined together, so think about where the join
    will be most inconspicuous. Often it's best to have the largest span of fabric in the middle
    with a small piece of fabric joined at each end.

2   As with almost all upholstery projects, the best place to start stripping off the old top cover
    is by turning the sofa upside down. This sofa has a slatted wooden deck rather than the usual
    jute webbing, which makes the seat a great deal stronger, but also much harder.

3 Use a tack, or in this case staple lifter, to free up the top fabric. Look out for signs of insect damage and any repairs that you may have to consider before reupholstering. The fine dust under the fabric shows obvious signs of woodworm activity, so the wood must be treated before any fabric is applied.

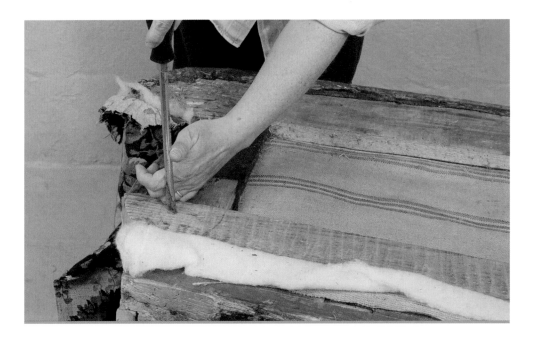

4 Once you have removed the outside back fabric, you can gain access to the screws holding the back to the main part of the sofa. Carefully undo the screws with a screwdriver that is appropriate for the job. Make sure you don't damage the screw heads or they will be difficult to remove and may need drilling out.

5   With the screws removed, the back can be carefully lifted off the main part of the sofa.

6   Once the two pieces of the sofa are separated, you will find that access to the rest of the arm and deck fabric is made possible. With a piece that is constructed in this way, stripping the old upholstery off is a very simple job.

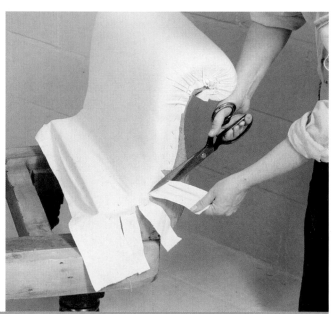

7   If necessary replace the old batting on the arms using your hands to break off the edges. Make sure they're thinned out and won't cause lumps under the new fabric.

8   Cover the new batting with a layer of muslin. Attach the muslin from side to side and then top to bottom, smoothing as you go so that it follows the shape of the arm curve. Trim off the excess, paying particular attention to the back edge. Make sure you don't impede the reattachment of the back of the sofa.

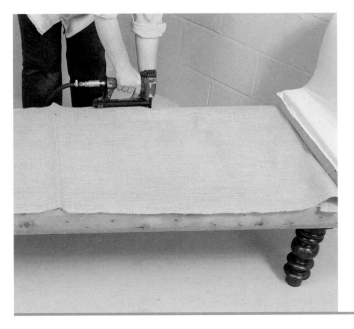

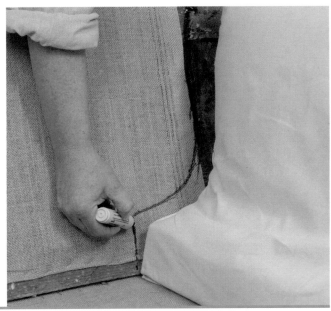

9 Cover the deck with a new piece of good quality burlap, folding the edges under as you go.

10 At this stage, hold the stripped back piece up to the sofa. Mark the line of where it will meet the arms, so that when it's re-covered you will know which area to avoid padding.

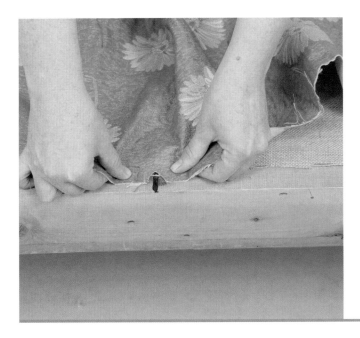

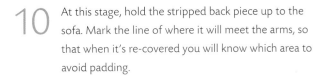

11 Measure the front edge of the deck and put a mark at the center point. Take the fabric you're going to cover the front edge of the deck in and fold it in half. Make a small snip in the front edge of the fold to mark the center point, turn the fabric upside down, and line it up with the center of the deck.

12 With a wide sofa, you will need to make the deck and back fabric out of two or more pieces, prepared beforehand. Take a length of tacking strip and attach it over the top of the deck fabric, so that it forms an invisible straight edge.

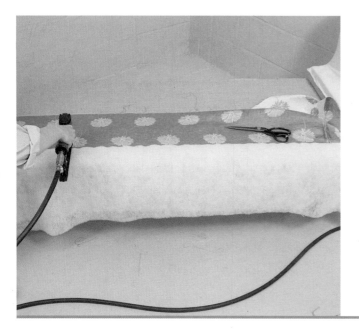

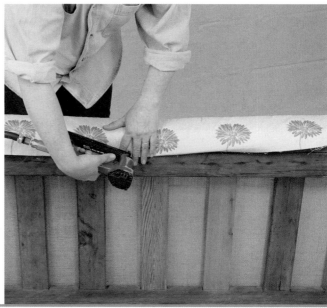

13   Fold a piece of Dacron in half to double its padding thickness. Attach it along the line of the tacking strip so that it pads the front edge of the deck.

14   Pull the deck fabric over the front edge of the deck and staple it underneath.

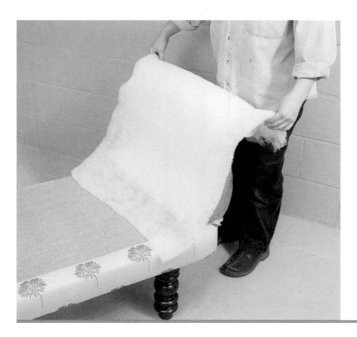

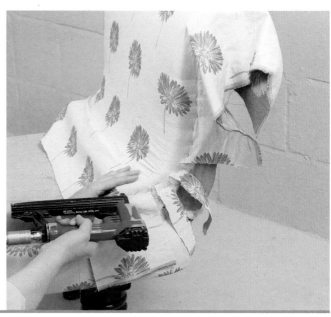

15   Re-cover the arms with a layer of Dacron.

16   Re-cover the arms with top fabric and secure it in the same manner as the muslin in Step 8, paying careful attention to smooth out any wrinkles.

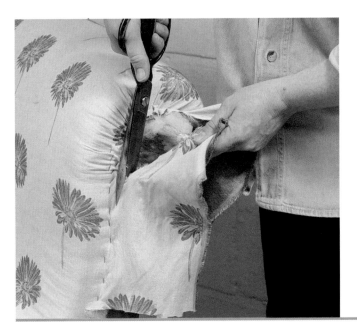

17 Trim off the excess fabric from the front and back of the arms, again making sure that there are no unnecessary lumps so that the back will fit on.

18 Turn the sofa upside down and attach the outside arm fabric under the lip of the arms using a staple gun and a length of tacking strip.

19 Add a little padding and protection between the outside arm fabric and wooden frame by applying a piece of synthetic fiber to the underside of the arms.

20 Pull the outside arm fabric over the outside arm and slowly staple it in place from side to side, so that it follows the line of the arm shape without wrinkling. Finish off by stapling the fabric to the underside of the deck. Once you've attached the outside arm fabric, finish off the front scrolls on the arms as shown in the Tools and Techniques section of this book (pp 44–45).

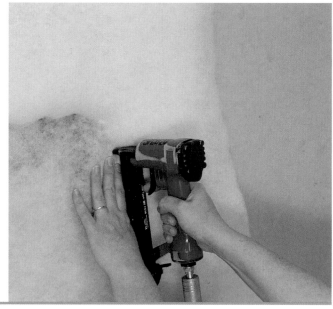

21 For the back, place batting over the whole of the back rest, except for the areas covered by the arms. Batting breaks apart easily and can be formed to the exact shape you want just by tearing it.

22 Because batting breaks apart so easily, it must always be covered by a thin layer of Dacron. Cover the front of the back with Dacron and staple it along the edge, where the back meets the back of the arms.

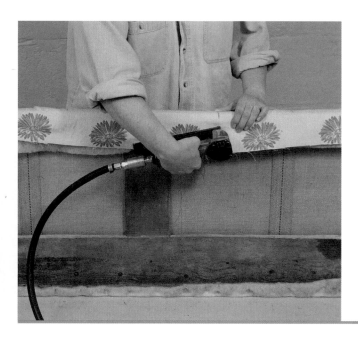

23 Cover the back with fabric and staple it in position. With a sofa as wide as this, the deck and back fabric is made from two or more pieces and prepared beforehand.

24 Position the covered back up to the sofa deck, and use a regulator to re-align the screw holes.

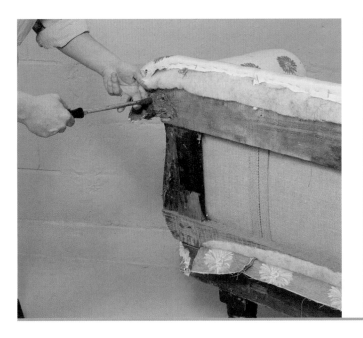

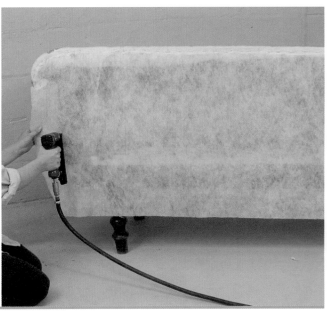

25   Carefully reattach the two parts of the sofa. If possible, use new screws and dab a little petroleum jelly on their threads so that they go in more easily and protect the screw holes in the wood.

26   Attach a piece of Dacron to the outside back to add a little padding and to stop the outside back fabric from rubbing against the wood on the frame.

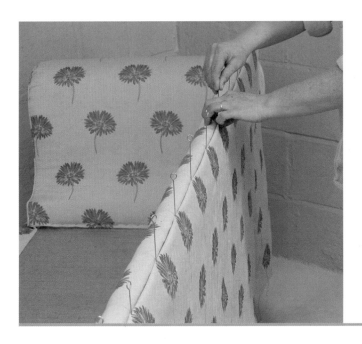

27   Attach the outside back fabric to the back of the sofa by folding the top edge under and pinning in place. Once the top edge is in place, staple the bottom edge under the deck and then continue pinning the outside edges in place.

28   Carefully hand-stitch the top and outer edges of the outside back fabric to the outside arm and back fabric, removing the pins as you go.

29 Fill in the two scroll arms using the techniques described on pages 44-45. Two bolster cushions add the final finishing touches. Find out how to make these in the Tools and Techniques section, pages 54–57.

BARREL CHAIR WITH SPLIT ARMS AND DECORATIVE NAILS

Before

The barrel-style chair is very practical and comfortable. This example dates from around 1930 and is upholstered in the traditional style, with a coil sprung seat and angular cabriole legs. Barrel chairs (or tub chairs) have a curved inner face, comprising back and arms, and it's this feature that causes most problems for the upholsterer. To cover the inner face of the chair, you must either use three pieces of fabric or apply deep buttoning to the back and arms, so that you can hide fabric joins in the folds between the buttons. This is why you often see buttoning on curved chairs. The chair for this project will be covered in plain fabric.

After

84

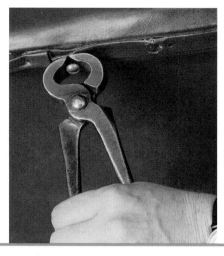

1   The first job is to remove the bottom cloth and expose the webbed and sprung base. Use a tack lifter to remove the tacks or staples that are securing the fabric on the outside of the back, arms, and front.

2   If you have dome head nails to deal with, you may find a pair of pliers easier to use than the tack lifter.

3   Continue to remove the staples, tacks, or nails holding the outside back, arm, and front fabric.

4   Under the outside back and arm fabric you'll usually find a supporting layer of burlap or muslin.

5   Once you have removed the burlap or muslin from under the outside arms and back, you will have access to all the rungs of the frame where the seat and inner surface fabric is secured.

6   With all the fabric removed, you can peel off any old batting and assess the condition of the old upholstery. You can decide whether to strip the chair back to the frame and completely reupholster in the traditional manner, or re-cover with batting and fabric.

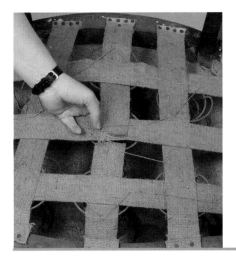

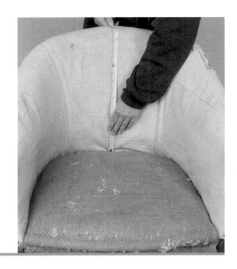

7 Turn the chair back over and carry out any necessary repairs to the underseat webbing. This chair's webbing was about to give way.

8 If the old webbing is still good enough to hold the coil seat springs in place, secure some new webbing over the top of it. This is always a good option if you don't want to try stitching springs into new webbing when you've only got small gaps in the webbing.

9 After addressing the sprung seat, turn the chair back onto its legs and measure up for its new cover. Either make a cutting plan on paper to cut out the fabric or use the old fabric as a template.

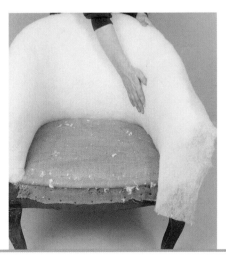

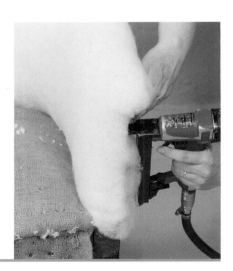

10 Apply a new layer of batting to the inside arms and back, shaping it over the tops of the back and arms as you go. Use your hands to tear the batting rather than using shears, as this gives a finer edge without leaving any lumps.

11 Once the batting is in place, lay a thin layer of Dacron over the top to stop it from being disturbed by the top fabric.

12 Secure the Dacron in place with a few staples around the edges.

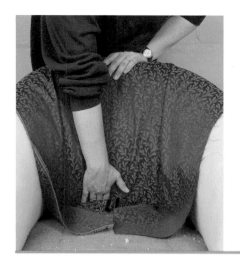

13 The back fabric goes on first. Lay it over the back and smooth it around the curve of the chair until it's positioned centrally.

14 Starting with the bottom, cut into the fabric at intervals of 3 or 4 inches so that it follows the curve of the seat rail and can be pulled around the back supports.

15 Tuck the fabric through and, making sure you smooth out any wrinkles as you go, pull the strips of fabric up around the seat rail one at a time and staple them in place.

16 When the bottom edge of the fabric is secure, smooth it up over the top of the chair and attach it to the underside of the top rail.

17 Make two lengths of piping long enough to reach from under the seat rail to up and over the top rail. Lay them over the fabric where the joins with the arm pieces are going to be.

18 Secure the bottom of the piping under the seat rail where the back leg is.

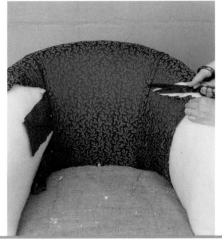

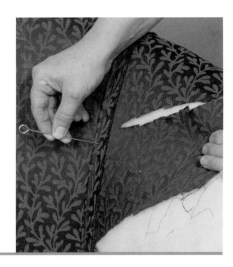

19 Then stretch the piping over the top rail and secure it under the frame.

20 Do this on both sides and then cut into the fabric that protrudes beyond the piping at regular intervals up to the piping. Do this so that the fabric can follow the inner curve of the chair without wrinkling.

21 Use upholstery pins to hold the piping and fabric together while you apply the arm fabric.

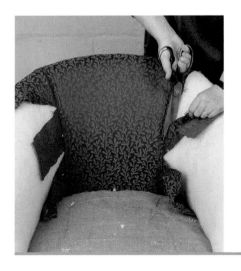

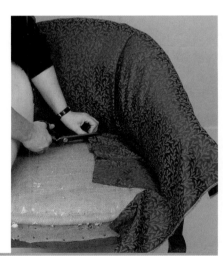

22 Trim off as much of the excess fabric as necessary to prevent the join between the back and arm fabric being lumpy, before you apply the arm fabric.

23 Place the arm fabric over the chair and spend some time smoothing and positioning it before making any cuts.

24 Cut into the bottom edge of the arm fabric where necessary to enable it to go around the chair frame.

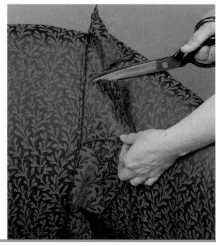

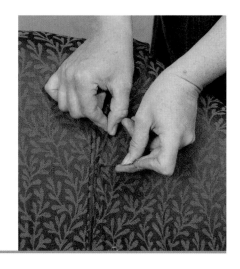

25 Secure the bottom edge of the fabric around the lower arm rung first and then smooth the fabric up and over the top rail before stapling underneath.

26 Peel back the side of the arm fabric where it overlaps the back fabric and make cuts into it up to the point where it meets the piping.

27 Fold the fabric under so that it makes a neat edge along the length of the piping. Use upholstery pins to hold the join between the fabric and piping together.

28 Using a small curved needle, slip stitch the back fabric, piping, and side fabric together along the length of the join. Remove the pins as you go.

29 Finally, pull the front edge of the arm fabric around the front of the chair frame and neatly fold and secure it at the side of the frame.

30 Once you have secured the fabric on both arms and back, it's time to do the seat. The first step is to put a layer of batting over the seat. Shape the front edge by breaking it apart with your hands.

31 Batting is likely to break up and be difficult to work with, so place a layer of thin Dacron over the top of it to keep it in place. Tuck it under the arms and back.

32 Lay your seat fabric over the batting and fleece and take your time positioning it before making any cuts. It needs to go around the chair frame, the back, and then the front of the arm.

33 Secure the front of the seat fabric to the front edge of the seat frame first.

34 Secure the back and sides of the seat fabric to the frame.

35 For the front seat bands make up a length of welting and machine-sew it along the top edge of a piece of fabric.

36 Place the welting in position just under the front edge of the seat. Lift it back over onto the seat and secure it in place with a length of tacking strip.

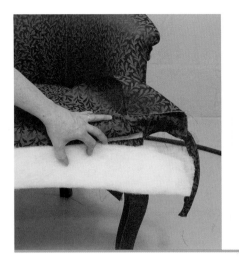

37 Fold some Dacron into a pad. Secure it over the tacking strip.

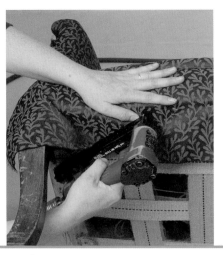

38 Pull the fabric over the Dacron pad and secure it under the front edge of the chair frame.

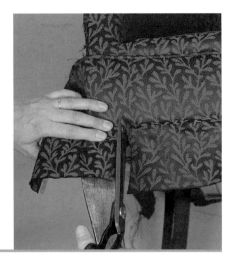

39 Finish the fabric around the tops of the legs by cutting up to the point where it meets the chair frame.

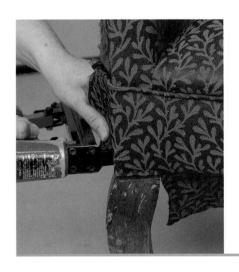

40 Fold the fabric under to form a neat line across the top of the leg and securing it at the side.

41 Attach some Dacron to the outside back and arms and trim it so that it doesn't protrude beyond the line of the fabric.

42 Position the outside back fabric first.

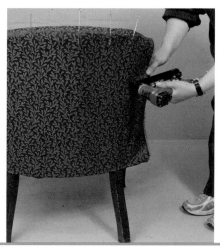

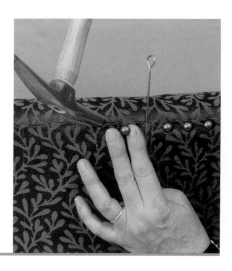

43 Make sure it's positioned correctly and then fold the top edge so that it follows a smooth line along the top of the chair. Secure the top with upholstery pins and then staple the bottom under the seat frame.

44 Fold the fabric under where it falls over the tops of the legs and attach it along the back rung at the sides.

45 Attach the top of the back fabric with a line of evenly spaced upholstery nails. Applying upholstery nails takes a little practice. Space them one or two inches apart and then fill in the gaps.

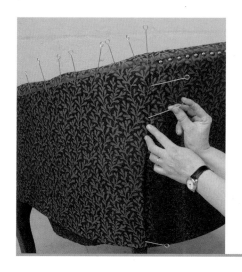

46 Apply the side fabric in the same way as the back. Use upholstery pins to attach the top edge. Fold the front and back edge into a nice straight seam and pin in place.

47 Attach the front side with a line of upholstery nails and continue on up the side and then down the back along the join between the outside back and side fabric.

48 Finally, cut out a piece of burlap or cambric, cut and fold its edges under, and secure it all around the underneath of the chair.

49 This classic 1930s chair, in its new finery, is as comfortable as it looks.

WING CHAIR WITH PIPING

Before

Wing chairs are armchairs with high backs and sides that were originally designed to support the head and shoulders while blocking out drafts. This style of chair has been popular since it was first made in the 18th century and remains so today. Fine antique wing chairs are much sought after and can fetch large sums of money. But they are hard to find. Museum-quality pieces are rare. However, a reproduction with some age and good bones may be found at an auction, a fair, or in an antique shop. If the price is right, the piece may be worth re-covering, like the example in this project.

After

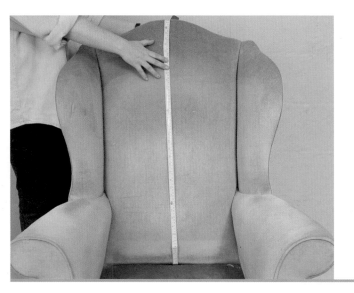

1 Take a good look at your chair before you get started on reupholstery. See how firm the upholstery is and whether the chair is suitable for re-covering, or if it's in too poor a condition to get involved. Take measurements and decide how much fabric the chair will need and what sort of fabric you want to cover it in.

2 Start by removing the bottom cloth to expose the tacks or staples, holding the outside arm back and seat fabric under the seat frame. Be alert all the time you're stripping off the old fabric for signs of insect damage that may require treating, or in extreme cases, may force you to abandon the project altogether.

3 Use scissors or a sharp knife to cut away any stitches that secure the fabric around the outside back and arms.

4 Work systematically to remove the fabric and muslin underneath, exposing more tacks and staples holding the inside arm, back, and seat fabric.

5   You'll find that the inside wing and back fabric will be attached to the inner part of the back frame, so work your way through the back webbing to free up any tacks or staples. If you need to remove one or two pieces of the webbing to gain access do so, but remember to replace it before you put the outside back fabric on.

6   The outside arm fabric will probably be attached under the arm with a tacking strip, which can be removed once you have freed up the fabric where it is attached under the seat.

7   Work systematically and you'll often find that the arm covers can be pulled back over the arms in one piece, if they're constructed that way.

8   With all the fabric freed from under the chair frame and from the back, the whole chair can be exposed by pulling the fabric out from where it's tucked in around the seat and back.

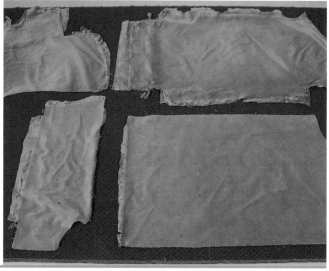

9   Because they've been popular for many centuries, wing chairs can be difficult to age. Often, you'll find the original chair fabric under a more recent cover, giving you an opportunity to make an educated guess by looking at the style of fabric the chair was covered in when new.

10   Strip the old fabric off carefully, so you can carefully lay it over your new fabric and use it as a guide to cutting out. Make sure to allow 3 or 4 inches excess all around to give you something to grip. (It must be admitted here that no professsional upholsterer would usually leave an old cover under fresh fabric.)

11   The deck is the starting place, and as there is a cushion, you need a piece of fabric with a seam 6 inches back from the front edge. Fold where you want the seam to go and stitch a length of webbing to it $1/2$ inch down from the fold. The webbing will act as a reinforcing piece and help you pull the seam down when attaching it to the deck rail.

12   Place a new layer of Dacron over the deck and tuck it in all round the sides and back, so that the new fabric won't rub over the old fabric or upholstery.

13   Take the deck fabric with the webbing reinforced seam and lay it over the deck with the back part of the fabric pulled over the front of the chair to give access to the webbing. Take some strong thread or buttoning twine and hand-stitch the webbing to the deck 6 inches in from the front.

14   With the seam stitched to the deck, fold the fabric back over and make cuts into the corners to allow it to fit around the frame at the back.

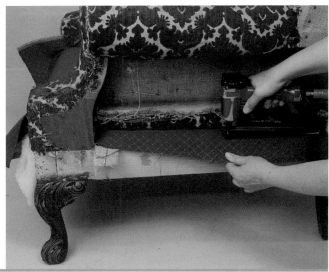

15   Make cuts into the sides just in from the front of the arms, so it fits around the frame at the front.

16   Pull the fabric through the frame at the sides and attach it to the top of the lower chair frame; do the same with the back.

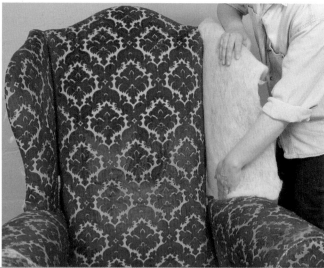

17 Attach the front seat fabric with neatly folded seams at the side edges, and then smooth it underneath the front edge and staple it in place.

18 The wings come next. Cover them with a layer of Dacron to prevent the new fabric from rubbing against the old. Hold it in place around the outside edges with a few staples.

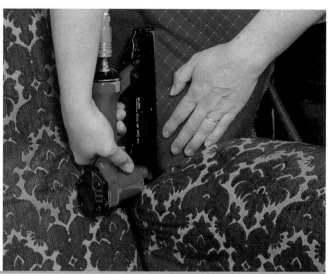

19 Place your fabric over the wing and take time to make sure it's correctly positioned before making any cuts. Put cuts in to allow it to fit around the frame on top of the arm.

20 Push down the upholstery on top of the arm where it joins the wing, tuck the new fabric down the gap, and make sure you staple it where the staples won't show.

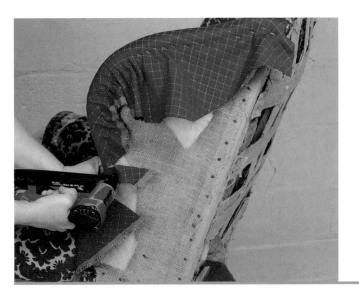

21 Neatly fold the wing fabric around the edges of the wing and make any cuts necessary to allow it to smoothly follow the curve of the wing, before stapling it in place.

22 Tuck the back of the wing fabric through the gap between the back. Go around to the back and pull the wing fabric through the gap so that it comes out the back. Staple it in place on the inside of the back frame.

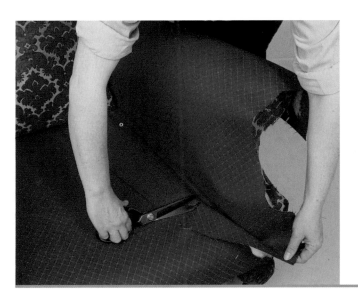

23 When you have done both wings, you can place your fabric over the arms. Place your fabric carefully and make cuts to allow it to fit around the arm frame before pulling it through and attaching it over the top of the seat fabric on the deck frame.

24 Smooth the arm fabric up and over the top of the arm and staple it underneath.

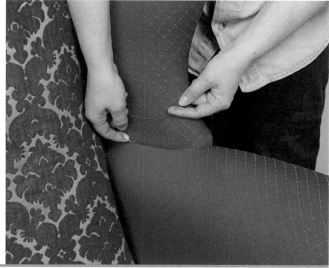

25 Pull the back of the arm fabric through the back of the chair and secure it the same way you did the back of the wing. Finally, fold the fabric neatly around the front scroll and staple it in place. Make small cuts where necessary to allow the fabric to follow the curve of the scroll.

26 Fold the part of the arm fabric under where it meets the bottom of the wings and carefully slip stitch between the two to form an unobtrusive seam.

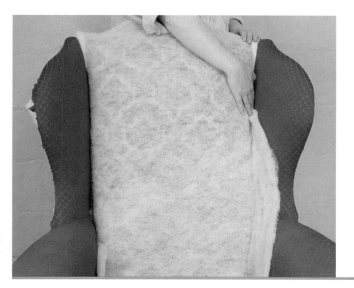

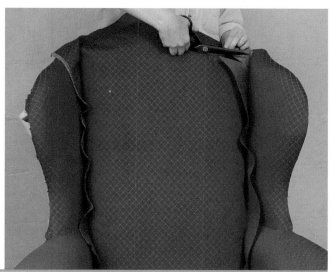

27 When you've finished both wings, lay Dacron over the back so the new fabric doesn't rub against the old and tuck it in neatly.

28 Place your back fabric over the Dacron and make any cuts that you need to tuck it around the frame at the top, bottom, and sides.

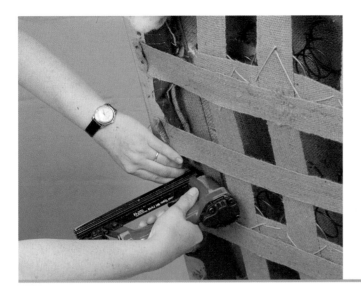

29 Tuck in the back fabric and pull it out through the back. Attach it through the webbing at the back, on top of the wing and arm fabric, and then re-attach any burlap and other original upholstery that you had to free to strip the old cover off.

30 Smooth the back fabric up and over the curve of the back. Staple it in place along the top of the frame.

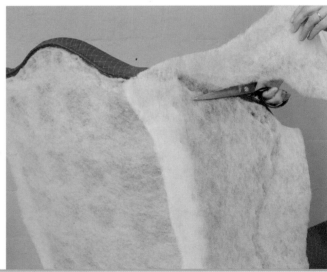

31 Make up sufficient welting to go around the edges of both wings and along the top of the back and carefully staple it in place to form an edging running all the way across from one side to the other.

32 Cover the open outside wings and back with Dacron and trim off the excess so it doesn't protrude past the welting edge.

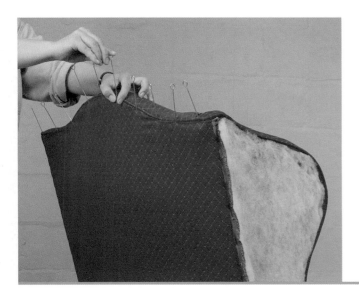

33 Apply the outside back fabric to the back. Once you have stapled the sides and bottom of the back fabric in place, fold the top edge under so that it makes a neat join along the curve of the welted edge. Use upholstery pins to hold it in place.

34 Do the same with the outside wing fabric. Fold and pin it in place where it meets the back fabric and welted edge along the front.

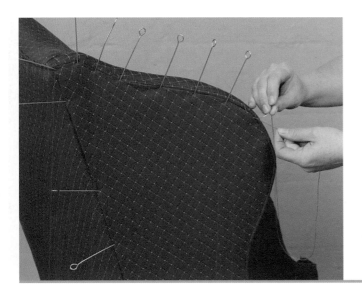

35 Slip stitch the wing fabric and top of the back to the welted edge and where the back and wing fabric meet, removing the pins as you go.

36 Turn the chair on its side and lay the outside arm fabric over the arm. Take a length of tacking strip and staple it to the outside arm fabric along the under side of the arm to form an invisible seam.

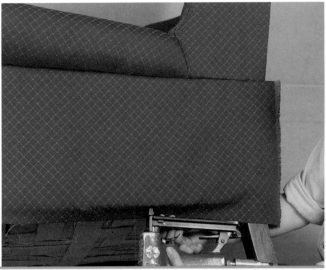

37 Place a layer of Dacron under the outside arm fabric to add a little padding and stop the fabric from rubbing against the bare wood of the frame.

38 Pull the outside arm fabric tight under the seat frame and staple it in place.

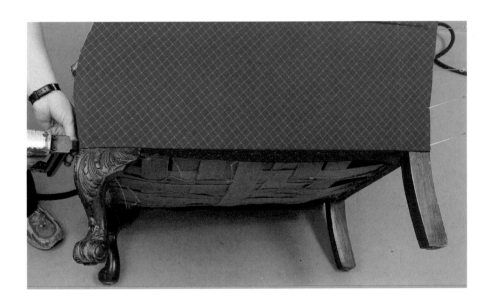

39 Cut and fold the outside arm fabric over the top of the chair legs front and back, and then secure it to the front edge of the arm and around the back of the frame.

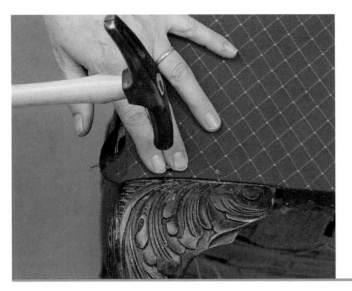

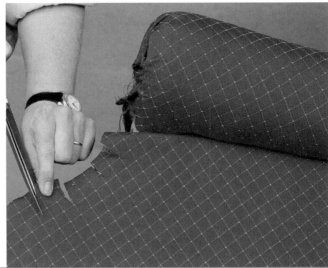

40 Use colored gimp pins to secure the folded fabric over the top of the chair legs.

41 Make cuts to the front edge of the outside arm fabric, so that it folds nicely around the curve of the arm scroll and staple it to the front of the arm.

42 Using the old arm fabric as a template if possible, make up a shaped front to the arm with welting sewn around the edge. Pad the inside of the scroll with a little batting.

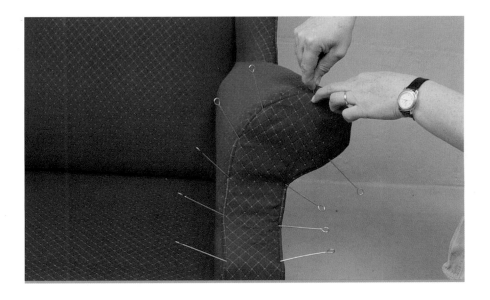

43 Use upholstery pins to hold the front arm piece in place.

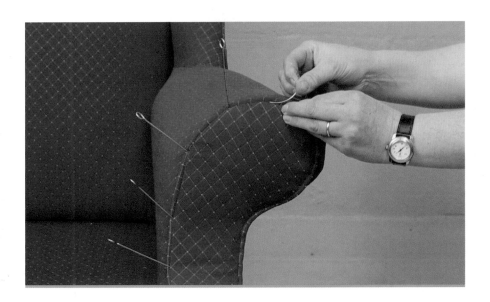

44 Finally, slip stitch the welted edge of the front arm to the arm fabric, removing the pins as you go.

45 Finally, re-cover the box cushion and add it as the finishing touch. See the Tools and Techniques section, pages 58–59, for how to make a box cushion.

ROUND-SHOULDERED T-CUSHION CLUB CHAIR

Before

The club chair is a classic design of armchair, originating in the mid-19th century. Still popular today, the chair can be upholstered with a tight seat and back, or with a loose seat cushion. The chair in this project dates from the early 20th century and has been recently renovated, so it looks like new. This project shows how to replace the top cover and change a tight seat into a seat with a box cushion in the simplest way. As the deck extends out and in front of the arms, the seat cushion will be a T-cushion made to the exact shape required.

After

1 Take your time going over the chair before making any changes. Make sure you know what it is you're going to do beforehand. To change the top fabric, remove the bottom cloth first so that you have access to the fabric under the chair frame. Remove the outside back fabric to allow access to the outside arm fabric.

2 Remove the tacks or staples, attaching the outside back fabric to the back chair rails. Snip through any stitches you find, removing the tacking strip from under the arm's roll.

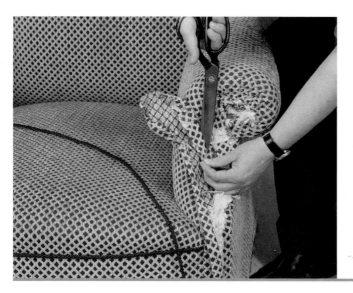

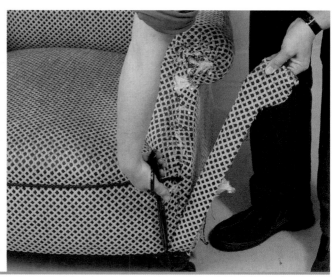

3 Before you can remove the outside arm fabric completely, you must remove the scroll on the front of the arms so that you can access the tacks or staples holding the front of the outside back fabric on.

4 Remove the scroll pieces carefully in case you want to use them as templates to cut out the new fabric.

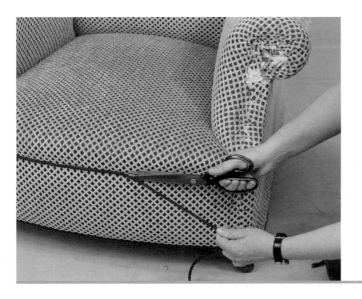

5   This chair was trimmed with decorative cord, which is easy to remove by snipping through the hand stitches.

6   Once the two scrolls and outside arm fabric are removed, the front panel can be taken off. Remove any old batting, but leave the stuffing alone; it's only the top cover that's being replaced, and you don't want to disturb the general shape of the upholstery.

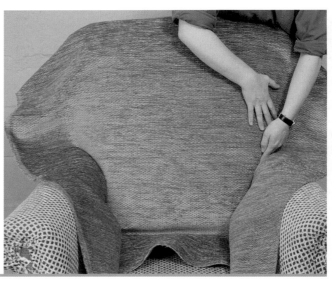

7   When replacing the top cover you can generally leave the old inside back, arm, and deck fabric in place. The first piece of fabric to apply is the back piece, so cover the old fabric with a layer of Dacron to stop it from sticking to the old fabric.

8   Lay the new fabric over the Dacron and take time lining it up before making any cuts.

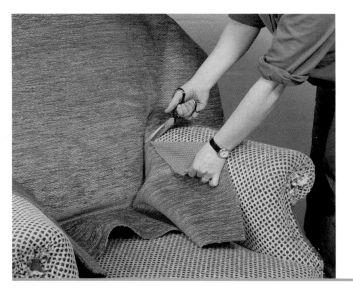

9   With the fabric placed correctly, make your first cuts into the sides where they meet the backs of the arms. Chair frames are all slightly different so the exact positioning of the cuts can only be determined by feeling into the join between the back and arms. Cut into the fabric only enough to allow it to go around the chair frame.

10   Tuck the parts of the fabric through the gap one piece at a time and then make further cuts if necessary. This will keep mistakes to a minimum and stop you from making cuts where they aren't needed and could possibly show.

11   Once you have tucked the sides of the fabric through to the back and down through the back of the seat, smooth the fabric up and over the back and staple it in place behind the frame.

12   Pull the bottom edge of the back fabric up over the bottom rail of the back frame and staple it in place.

13 Staple the fabric tucked through between the arm and the back to the side of the chair frame and trim off the excess fabric, so it doesn't leave any lumps.

14 Finally, staple the fabric around the sides of the back, making sure that you keep the fabric smooth and wrinkle free.

15 Finish the top corners by carefully folding the fabric so that it lies unobtrusively along the middle of the corner curve.

16 Pull the fold up tight and staple the fold in place behind the chair frame at the back.

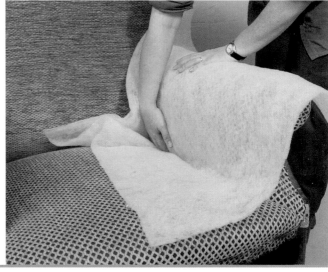

17 Carefully snip off any excess fabric, so that the folds don't make lumps under the outside back fabric when it's replaced.

18 The arms are covered next, so leave the inside arm fabric in place and cover it with a layer of Dacron. This prevents any chafing on the inside of the new fabric.

19 Lay the arm fabric over the arms and make sure that the pattern or texture lines up with the direction of the back fabric before making any cuts.

20 Push your hand in between the arm and back to establish where you will have to make cuts, and to allow the fabric to go around the frame. Carefully cut into the back edge and tuck the fabric through.

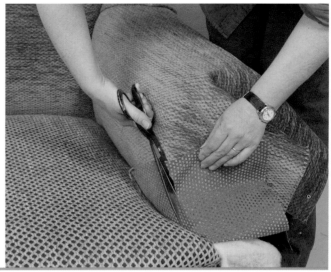

21 Do the same where the bottom of the arm fabric tucks into the seat. Carefully make whatever cuts are necessary to allow it to tuck through and out the side.

22 Make the cuts one at a time and tuck as much fabric in as you can after each cut, so that you avoid any irreversible mistakes.

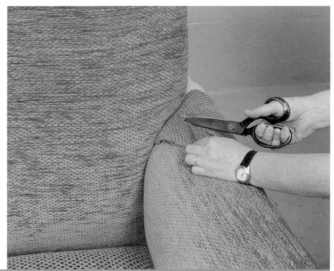

23 When you tuck the fabric in make sure you keep it positioned correctly and aligned.

24 Wait until all the main cuts are made before adding the last one or two to the more fiddly areas, such as the top of the arm at the back and the very front of the seat.

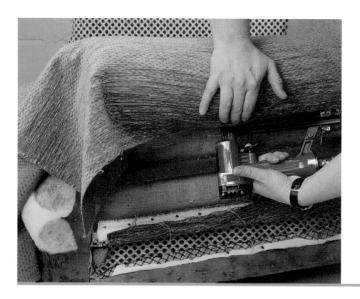

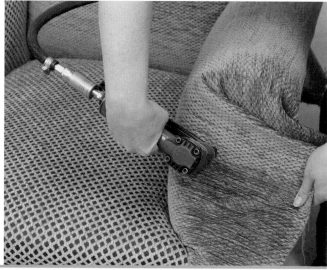

25   Staple the bottom edge of the inside arm fabric to the bottom arm rail. Smooth it up and over the roll of the arm and staple it underneath.

26   Pull the front edge of the inside arm fabric over the front of the arm and carefully staple it in place.

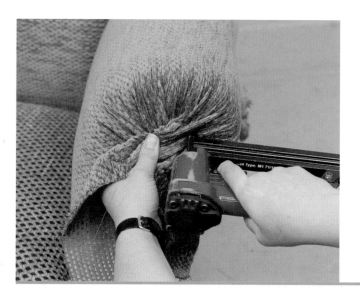

27   Continue stapling around the whole of the front of the arm, allowing small pleats so that the fabric remains straight as it follows the curve of the scroll.

28   Trim off the excess fabric from around the scroll.

29 Staple the back edge of the arm fabric so that it lays flat against the back rail.

30 Finally, on the arms, staple the fabric that tucks through the back of the arm on to the side of the back rail.

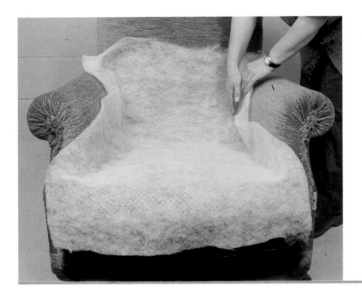

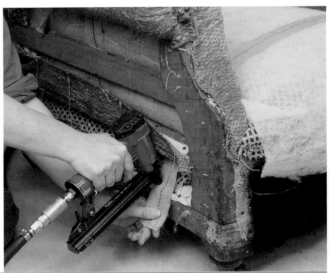

31 Once you've finished the inside arms the seat is next. The first thing to do is lay a piece of Dacron over the seat fabric. To turn a tight seat without a cushion into a deck you must alter its shape slightly.

32 A quick way is to place a webbing strap over it. Take a length of jute webbing and secure one end to the top of the bottom rail of the chair frame just behind the front of the arm frame. (Strictly speaking, you should reduce the seat padding to maintain the correct height; but the webbing strap method is much easier.)

33 Run the webbing over the seat in a straight line to the other side and tuck it down between the bottom of the arm and seat. Pull it tight so it compresses the seat slightly and forms a pronounced dip between the front third of the deck and the rear two thirds. Then staple it to the top of the bottom rail. The seat has now become a deck.

34 Lay the deck fabric over the deck and ensure that it runs in the same direction as the back and arm fabric, and that any pattern is positioned where you want it to be.

35 Fold the front of the deck fabric back so that it forms a fold over the top of the webbing strap. Stitch the fabric and webbing together over the top of the deck.

36 Pull the front of the deck fabric back over the front. Tuck the back and sides of the deck fabric in, making cuts as necessary, and secure them to the top of the bottom rail.

37 Smooth the front of the deck fabric forward and over the lip of the deck. Hold the fabric in place under the lip with upholstery pins.

38 Carefully hand-stitch the front edge of the deck fabric under the lip and remove the pins as you go.

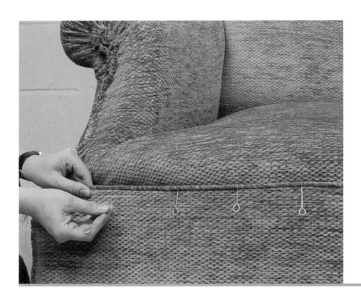

39 Make up a front panel, or front seat band, by sewing welting to the edge of your front fabric, or if you're going to use decorative cord to finish off, you can just fold the top edge under. Pin the front panel in place in a straight line under the lip of the deck.

40 Slip stitch the top of the front panel to the front of the deck fabric and remove the pins as you go.

41 Pull the front panel up over the deck and put a new piece of Dacron or batting over the stuffing at the front.

42 Pull the front panel back over the front of the chair, smooth it under the bottom frame, and staple it in place. Start in the middle and work your way out to the sides.

43 When you get to the legs make a cut into the fabric and fold it over the top of the show wood. Make sure that any staples you put in to hold the fabric over the leg will be covered by the new arm scroll fabric.

44 All that's left is to replace the outside back and arm fabric before restitching the scrolls. Start with the outside arms; turn the chair onto its side and lay the outside arm fabric over the roll of the arm with its inside facing out. Lay a piece of tacking strip over it on the underside of the arm roll.

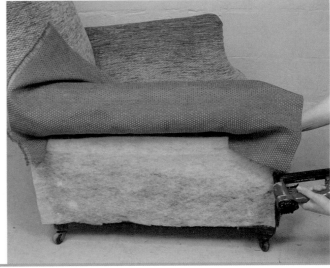

45 Because there are many layers of fabric on top of the wood of the frame, you may want to use upholstery tacks to hold the tacking strip on instead of staples.

46 Leave the outside arm fabric draped over the arm roll and staple a layer of Dacron to protect the underside of the fabric.

47 Pull the outside arm fabric down and staple it to the underside of the bottom rail, then the back of the back rail and finally around the front arm scroll.

48 Staple a piece of Dacron to the back of the chair to protect the underside of the back fabric and then trim off any excess.

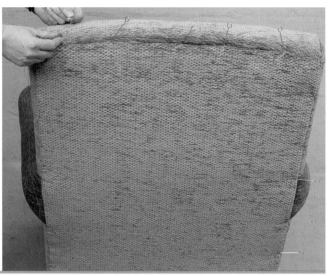

49   Attach the outside back fabric to the back of the chair by folding its top edge under and pinning it in place, then do the same with the sides and staple the bottom edge under the bottom rail.

50   Slip stitch the top and sides of the back fabric all around the back of the chair, removing the pins as you go.

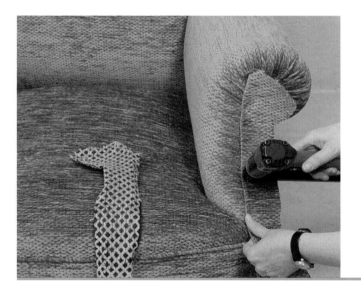

51   Using the old scroll pieces as a template, cut out new scroll pieces. Fold the edges of the fabric under and staple them in place on the front of the arms.

52   Finish off by slip stitching decorative cord over the heads of the staples holding the scrolls on.

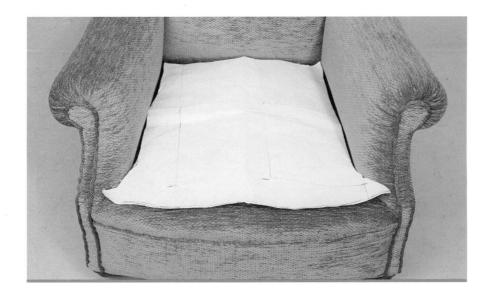

53　Make a template for the seat cushion by laying a piece of paper over the deck and cutting it to the exact shape.

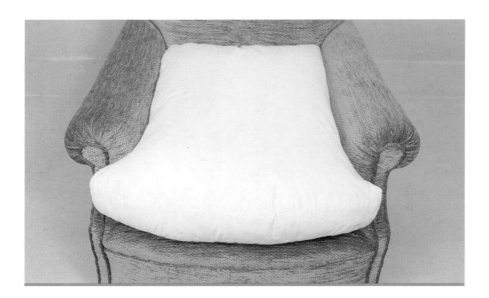

54　If you're going to make an irregular shaped seat cushion, then any inner for the seat cushion filling must of course be the same shape as the outer.

55   Here you can see that making a template is the only way to ensure that the seat cushion fits the exact shape of the deck.

TUB CHAIR WITH TUFTED BACK

Before

The low, tub style of chair used in this project used to be referred to as a nursing chair. The design dates back to the late 18th century and is a comfortable and relaxing shape that has changed little since and still remains popular today. At first glance, the project chair looks to be an original example, but it is in fact a modern reproduction upholstered with preformed foam padding. Modern chairs like this are excellent re-covering projects, as the upholstery retains its shape even when the top cover is removed. There's no need to be intimidated by the thought of re-covering a modern deep buttoned chair. This project illustrates that such pieces can be approached with confidence as long as you're prepared to remove the old fabric carefully to use as a template for the new cover.

After

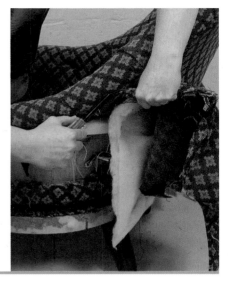

1 Remove the top cover by turning the chair over and taking off the dust cloth to expose the staples, securing the outside back arms and front fabric to the underside of the chair frame. Go carefully near any show wood, such as the legs. You don't want to cause any damage.

2 You often find that decorative nails are put on for show, so you'll still have to remove staples from underneath them before the fabric comes free.

3 Remove all the staples or tacks holding the fabric in place under the chair frame and then turn it back on to its feet. Remove the staples, tacks, or stitches holding the outside back and arm fabric on. If they are covered in one piece, the removal is more straightforward.

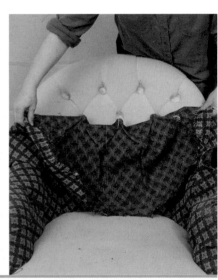

4 Once the fabric from the outside back and arms is removed, you will be able to remove the tacks and staples holding the seat fabric to the seat rails. Make sure you've removed them all and then pull the seat fabric out in one piece.

5 Carefully cut through the buttoning twine holding the buttons in place around the back and sides of the chair.

6 After cutting through all the buttoning twine and removing the tacks and staples from around the sides of the back and arm fabric, carefully pull the fabric away from the upholstery underneath. The chair is usually covered using three pieces of fabric; one for the back and one each for the arms.

7 With modern reproduction furniture, you will find that the shape of the chair and all the button placements have been perfectly preserved in the preformed foam padding underneath the top fabric.

8 Position the old inside back and arm fabric over the top of your new fabric, so that any pattern or texture is the right way round. Draw around the old fabric, allowing 2 or 3 inches extra, and then carefully mark where the button positions are.

9 With a dot representing the position of each button, remove the fabric template and cut out your new piece of inside back fabric. Do the same with the two arm pieces.

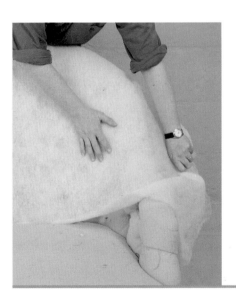

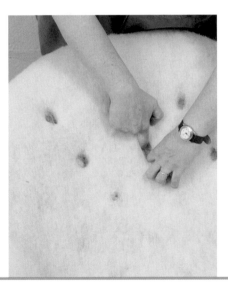

10 Cover the inside back and arms with a new layer of Dacron to stop the foam padding rubbing against the new top fabric and being worn away. Just smooth the Dacron over the foam and use a few staples to hold it in place.

11 You should be able to see where the buttons go through the Dacron. If not, feel where they are and push your fingers through the Dacron to open up a hole for the buttons to sink into.

12 Keep going until you've accounted for all the button positions in the back and arms.

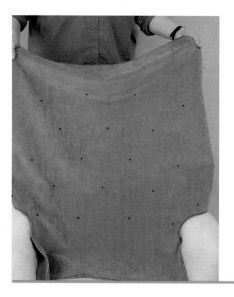

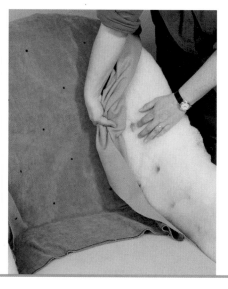

13 Carefully position the inside back fabric over the Dacron on the back of the chair, ready for buttoning.

14 Line the fabric up by making sure that the button positions marked on the fabric correspond with the same button positions on the chair.

15 Next you will need new buttons, lengths of buttoning twine, a double-ended needle, and pieces of webbing or other strong fabric to tie the back of the twine to.

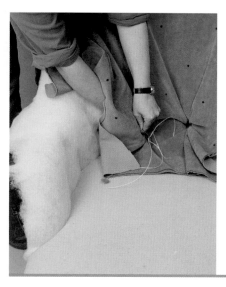

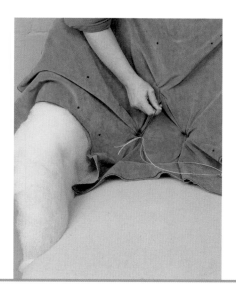

16 Buttoning is shown in detail in Tools and Techniques, pages 46–47. Line up the button position marked on the fabric, which represents the middle button on the bottom row, with the corresponding hole in the Dacron and insert your first button.

17 Finish the bottom row of buttons on the back, and then move up to the next row. Start with the middle button, and then the buttons on either side until that row is finished. Then do the same for the next row and so on.

18 After each completed row of buttons, slip your hand under the fabric and carefully re-establish the folds, joining one row of buttons to the other. Make sure you form the folds so that they face downwards; if they face up they will be more likely to collect dust.

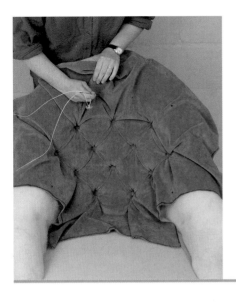

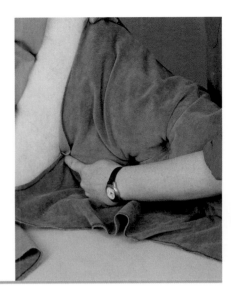

19 Finish all the back buttons first, before moving on to the arms.

20 Position the arm fabric over the arms and button them in exactly the same way as you did the back. Start with the middle button on the bottom row, finishing that row before moving up to the next row.

21 Two or three button positions on the back edge of the arm fabric will overlap with the same buttons on the edges of the back fabric. These can be joined so that it looks as if the back and arms are covered in one continuous piece of fabric.

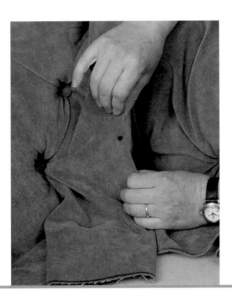

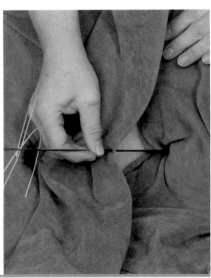

22 Make sure you're dealing with the same button position on both the back and arm fabric, and then cut into the edge of the back fabric in a straight line towards the button mark. Cut carefully into the fabric until you are about a $1/4$ inch away from the button mark.

23 Take the fabric from either side of the button mark and fold it under.

24 Thread your buttoning needle with a button in the usual way and push it through the button position on the back piece, the corresponding position on the arm piece, and through the button position on the chair.

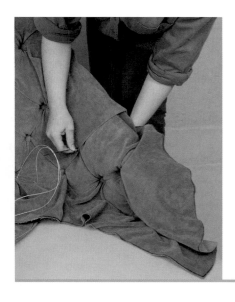

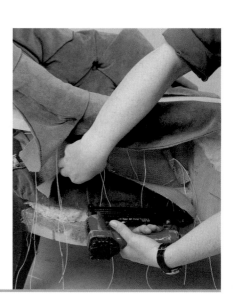

25   You will find that the fabric and arm fabric will overlap perfectly. The edge of the back fabric can be folded under to exactly match the other folds between the rows of buttons, making an invisible join.

26   Finish all the buttoning on the back and both arms before moving on.

27   Make cuts into the bottom edge of the back fabric to allow it to go around the frame at the back and sides, and tuck it through the edge of the seat.

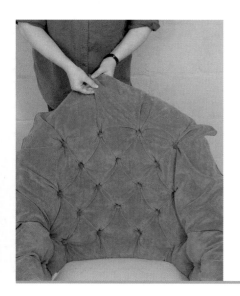

28   Take hold of the fabric in a line from each of the top buttons along the back and arms, and form a fold.

29   Hold the folds in place and secure the arm and back fabric in place under the lip of the top edge of the chair.

30   Repeat Step 28 for the bottom edge of the back and arm fabric and secure the bottom edge of the back and arm fabric under the chair rails.

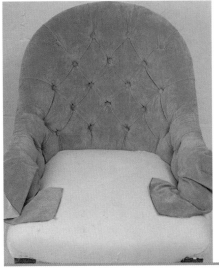

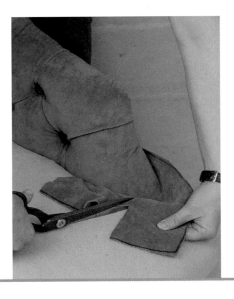

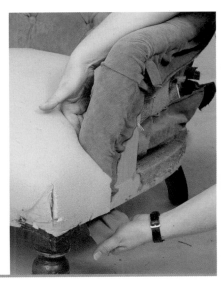

31 Leave the fronts of the arms until last.

32 Cut into the fabric at the front of the arms so that it will go around the front of the arm frame.

33 Tuck the very front section of arm fabric all the way through between the seat and secure it under the chair frame.

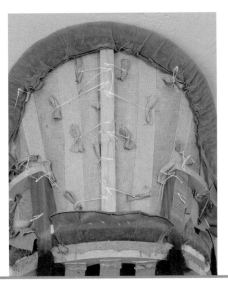

34 Return to the back of the chair, pull all the lengths of buttoning twine tight, and staple them to the chair frame to hold them in position.

35 It doesn't matter where you staple the buttoning twine: it's simply to keep it tight so the buttons hold the inside back and arms firm.

36 Once the inside back and arms are completely finished, the seat can be covered. Start by tucking a layer of Dacron over the seat foam.

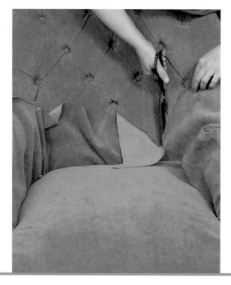

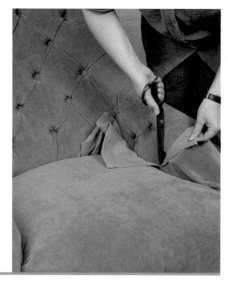

37 Position the seat fabric over the seat and ensure that any pattern or texture matches the back and arms before making any cuts.

38 Provisionally smooth the fabric over and tuck it down the side of the seat just to hold it in place. Cut into the back edge where it will have to go around the frame.

39 Tuck the back edge through between the back and seat first, before moving around toward the front to make more cuts.

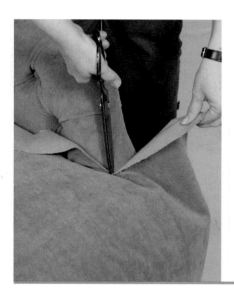

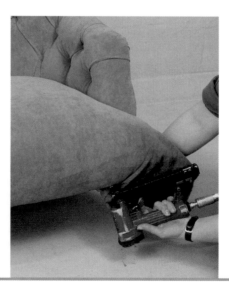

40 Again, keep tucking the fabric through after each cut to make sure it's in the right place and deep enough, before feeling down the edge of the seat for the next piece of frame to be negotiated.

41 Smooth the front edge of the seat fabric over the front, pull it under the chair frame, and staple it in place.

42 Make a cut into the fabric where it meets the leg. Do the same on the other side.

43 The front corners of the seat above the feet can be finished with a miter, as shown in the Tools and Techniques chapter, pages 50–53.

44 Attach a piece of Dacron to the outside back and arms, trimming it up so it doesn't protrude above the lip on the top of the chair.

45 Take your outside back and arm fabric, turn the top edge under, and use a few pins to hold it in place along the top lip of the chair. Staple the bottom edge of the back fabric under the frame. Hold the top edge of the fabric with more pins.

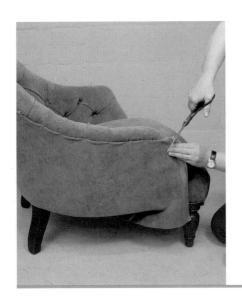

46 Make a few cuts into the front edge of the outside arm fabric so that you can turn it under and pin it in place along the sharp curve at the front of the arm.

47 Slip stitch the outside back and arm fabric to the inside back and arm fabric all along the length of the chair.

48 Finally, finish the top of the legs with an appropriate trimming. Here double piping held on with blue gimp pins is used, but you could just as easily use braid, gimp, or other trimming, stitched on or glued.

49 The finished chair will show all the signs of a professional upholsterer, especially the buttoning technique.

LOOSE-CUSHION SOFA WITH A BOX PLEATED SKIRT

Before

This sofa has a plain, contemporary design dating from the late 1960s. Loose cushions and relatively thin, simple arms give this sofa a very broad seating area. Though not very complicated, at 7 feet wide, it does take some time and a little bravery to attempt a re-covering job on this scale. But if you're skilled at sewing, take heart—half the time in recovering a sofa like this is taken up making new cushion covers. Unfortunately, the other half of the work requires a great deal of space and strength as you're going to have to turn the sofa over and lift it up on trestles to reach some of the places you need to get to.

After

1 It doesn't matter whether you're recovering a small chair or a 7-foot long sofa, the first thing to do is to remove the dust cover. Turn the sofa onto its back and start removing the staples or tacks holding it in place.

2 Once the dust cover is off, you can remove the tacks or staples holding on the outside arms and back. You can leave a lot of the old fabric in place, but you'll have to remove the seat fabric, and that can only be done once the outside arms and back are off.

3 The inside arm and back fabric can stay on, but you will have to detach their bottom edges to get to the staples holding the seat fabric in place.

4 Once the seat fabric is removed, lay a new layer of Dacron over the deck to protect the old upholstery and prevent the new top cover from rubbing against it.

5 Attach a new length of webbing over the deck about a third of the way in from the front edge. Run the webbing from one side of the frame to the other and tighten it slightly so it makes a slight trough, which will help hold the seat cushions in place.

6 With a sofa this size, the fabric is going to be a major expense. The deck is covered by cushions so make up the deck piece with a piece of inexpensive neutral fabric or muslin so that only the front third of the deck is covered.

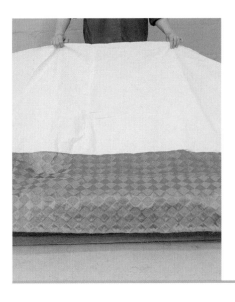

7   Lay the deck fabric on the deck and take your time positioning it so that the pattern is where you want it to be and you have enough excess fabric to attach to each side of the frame.

8   Don't tuck anything in at this stage, just fold the front third of the fabric back on itself along the line of the webbing and stitch the deck fabric to it.

9   Unfold the front third of the deck fabric over the front edge and start making the cuts you need into the side of the fabric so that it can be tucked around the frame.

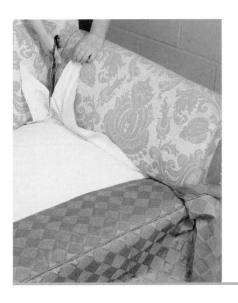

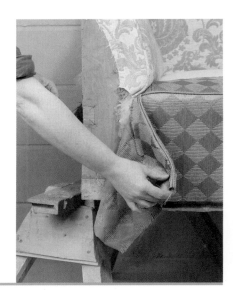

10   The main areas you'll need to cut into are the rear corners and up near the front of the arm.

11   The deck fabric is made so that a length of welting joins the front facing fabric with the fabric on the deck. It's important that the welting runs straight along the angle of the deck edge. If you have a feature that must be in a certain position, secure it first.

12   Turn the sofa on its back to access the underside of the frame, or raise it up on trestles. Once the front of the deck fabric is secured, go to the back and attach the back edge to the frame. Put a little tension on the fabric so it is without wrinkles.

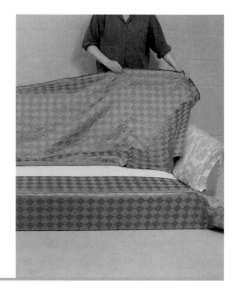

13 Attach the sides of the deck fabric.

14 Leave the sides of the fabric at the front unattached; you'll need to tuck the front of the arm fabric under these when you come to recover the arms.

15 The inside back fabric is next. Lay a piece of Dacron over the top of the old fabric to protect the new, and then position the new fabric over the top.

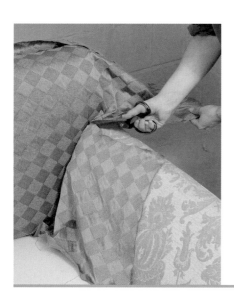

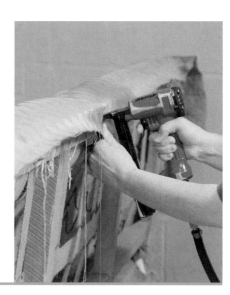

16 Once the back fabric is in the right place, so that any pattern is centralized and any texture flows in the same direction as the seat, make your first cuts into the bottom and outside edges so that you can tuck it around the frame at the back.

17 Tuck the back fabric through the seat and out the back of the frame. Tuck the sides through the gap between the arm and back frame and staple it to the side of the back frame.

18 Trim off any excess so that there's no bulky fabric causing lumps over the frame.

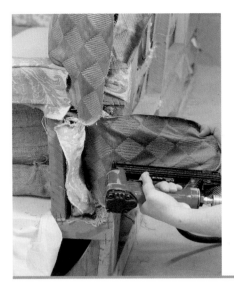

19   Pull the bottom edge of the deck fabric out the back and secure it to the seat rail.

20   Finally, smooth the inside back fabric up and over the top edge of the back. Staple it in place at the back of the frame.

21   To finish off the back corners, work your way toward them with the staple gun along from the middle of the top edge and up from the arm. Work out with a few practice folds how you can best finish the corner.

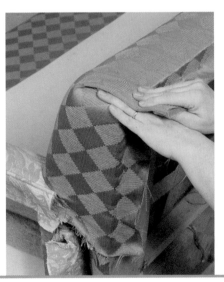

22   Just like gift wrapping, smooth the fabric up from the side.

23   Make a fold in the excess fabric and take it back over the corner, so that the fold rests unobtrusively on the apex of the angle.

24   Pull the fold tight and staple it in place behind the frame.

25 When the back fabric has been stapled all around, remember to reattach the old fabric over the top of it along the lower back and side rails.

26 Lay a new piece of Dacron over the arms.

27 Take time to position the arm fabric before you start making any necessary cuts, and tuck it around the back and seat frame.

28 Make your cuts one at a time and tuck as much fabric in as you can before moving on to make the next cut; this way you'll keep errors to a minimum and spot if you've inadvertently moved the fabric out of line before you go too far.

29 Pull the bottom edge of the arm fabric through between the seat and attach it to the bottom arm rail.

30 Staple the top edge of the inside arm fabric to the outside of the top arm rail. Work your way from the middle out to each end, but leave yourself room at the ends so you can decide how to finish them.

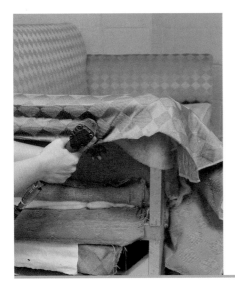

31 After making a few practice folds to check positioning, finish the back with a tight fold stapled to the side of the back frame.

32 Pull the front edge of the inside arm fabric around the front of the arm and staple it up towards the top corner.

33 Before you finish the top corner of the arm, pull the sides of the front fabric back and staple the bottom front of the arm fabric to the front edge of the sofa.

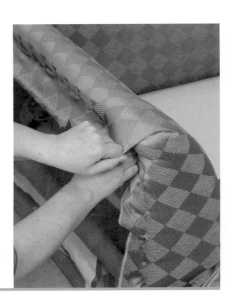

34 Finish the top corner of the arm in the same manner as you did the top back corner. Take the excess and pull the fabric tight over the corner.

35 Smooth the fabric over and decide where to make the fold.

36 Pull the fold tight and take it over the outside of the arm frame.

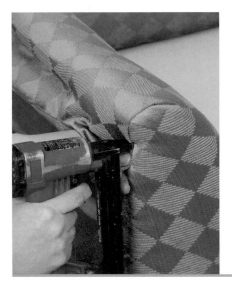

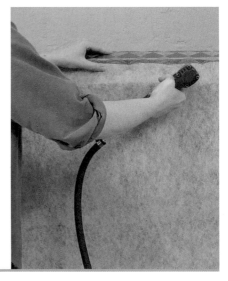

37 Hold the tension and staple the fold in place.

38 Pull the sides of the front fabric that you left loose in Step 14 over the top of the arm fabric and staple them to the sides of the frame.

39 All that's left is to replace the outside back and arm fabric and attach a new skirt. Staple a new piece of Dacron to the back of the sofa.

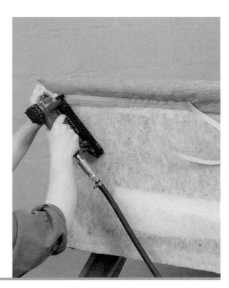

40 Lay the outside back fabric upside down over the inside back, so only the top edge comes over the top of the back, and carefully staple a length of tacking strip over the top edge.

41 Pull the outside back fabric over the top of the back and secure it underneath the bottom edge of the frame. Then staple a new piece of Dacron over the outside arms.

42 In the same way you did the outside back fabric, lay the outside arm fabric upside down over the inside arm, so that the top edge comes over the top of the arm. Staple a length of tacking strip over the top of it.

43 Pull the outside arm fabric over the outside arm and staple it under the bottom of the frame.

44 Staple the back edge of the outside arm fabric to the back edge of the back frame.

45 Fold the side of the outside back fabric under and pin it in place over the back and the outside arm fabric.

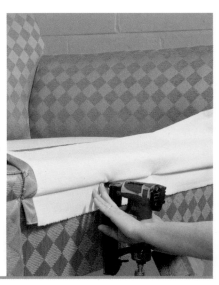

46 Slip stitch the seam along the back corner. Then turn the front edge of the outside arm fabric under, pin it in place, and slip stitch the front corner seam.

47 To make up the four skirt pieces, back the top fabric with muslin and a stiffener if required. Pin two of the skirt pieces in place along the front and on each side.

48 Make sure you leave a gap between the middle edges of the front skirt pieces and at the front corners, between the side and front pieces. Lift the skirts up and staple them in place.

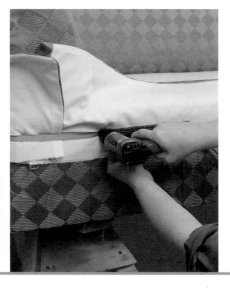

49 Add a small filler piece to the join between the front skirt pieces and one on each of the front corners, between the front and side pieces.

50 Finally, staple a length of tacking strip over the top of all four skirt pieces and three filler pieces where they attach to the sofa.

51 Drop the skirt back down and start making the new cushion covers.

52 The finished sofa looks fantastic and is as good as a new one, with its contemporary style.

Index

Page references in **bold** refer to projects.

METRIC CONVERSION CHART

1/4 inch	6mm
1/2 inch	12mm
3/4 inch	1.75cm
1 inch	2.5cm
2 inches	5cm
3 inches	7.5cm
4 inches	10cm
6 inches	15cm
9 inches	23cm
12 inches	30cm
1 yard	0.914m